Multicultural Europe

Number 2

Enid Gordon and Morwenna Jones

Portable Roots

Voices of Expatriate Wives

Presses Interuniversitaires Européennes
Maastricht

CIP-GEGEVENS KONINKLIJKE BIBLIOTHEEK, DEN HAAG

Gordon, Enid

Portable Roots : Voices of Expatriate Wives : by Enid Gordon
and Morwenna Jones. - Maastricht : Presses Interuniversitaires
Européennes. - (Multicultural Europe).
With ref., index.
ISBN 90-5201-011-0
SISO 328.9 UDC 3-054.72-055.2
Subject heading : Expatriate Wives : Europe.

P.I.E.
Hoogbrugstraat 45a,
6221 CP Maastricht,
The Netherlands.

To 'trailing spouses' present, past and future

CONTENTS

ACKNOWLEDGEMENTS

We would like to thank all the people who have helped to make this book possible.

In particular, for their inspiration, involvement and support, Maria João Pena, Huguette Rachel Nacmias, Norman MacKenzie and Judith Cottave, who all made vital contributions at different stages in the book.

Among the many others who have helped us, we must mention Barbara Cummings, Jeanne Daykin, Ann Devis, Joan Drape, Florence Gérard, Elizabeth Gordon, Jane Hartley, Bette Rose and Jorgen Heinø, Claudia Herstatt, Lydia Horton, Jill Hughes, Darah Lerner, Dr Maurice Lipsedge, Flora Pedlar, Maria Saradaki, Linda Steffey, Angela Veglianti and Pat Zanger. Their collective support and encouragement, and that of many others we have no space to mention, kept us going to the bitter end.

Our thanks are also due to expatriate clubs and associations and the staff of multinational companies, diplomatic services, other organizations too numerous to name and various publications, especially The Bulletin *(Brussels) and* Der Kontakt *(Brussels) for their help and the information they supplied.*

We thank, too, our publisher, Gaby Fragnière, and our editor, Margaret Haffenden, for their advice and their belief in the book, and our husbands, André Kirchberger and Hywel Jones, who bore with fortitude, patience and humour our four-year obsession with expatriate women.

Last but not least, our thanks go to all those women whose voices are heard in these pages and without whom this book could not have been written.

...There is, it seems to us,
At best, only a limited value
In the knowledge derived from experience.
The knowledge imposes a pattern, and falsifies,
For the pattern is new in every moment
And every moment is a new and shocking
Valuation of all we have been.

T.S. Eliot,
East Coker, from *The Four Quartets*,
London 1940

I

THREE WOMEN

FIONA

Fiona is British, 39, and lives in Paris with her son Peter.

Fiona and John met at university and married the week after they came down from Oxford. Like many of their friends, they settled in London, which, in the late 1960s, was, as she says, 'not a bad place to be in'. John became a civil servant and Fiona, who had always wanted to work in publishing, found herself a job in the editorial department of a small publishing house. Both their jobs made direct use of their qualifications and both paid the same - £2000 per annum. This was a promising start for bright young Oxbridge graduates, and very much what they had expected.

Perhaps it was too much what they had expected, for when Fiona saw an advertisement in *The Economist* for an interesting-sounding job at the O.E.C.D. (Organization for Economic Cooperation and Development) in Paris, she did not hesitate.

'I immediately suggested John try for it. I wonder why it never occurred to me to try for it myself. I was as well-qualified as he, after all. It simply never crossed my mind. When he was actually offered the job, I was delighted at the prospect of going to Paris. Both of us spoke quite good French. I thought it would be stimulating and the salary seemed enormous - it was far bigger than our two salaries put together. So I was totally in favour and gave up my job in publishing, confident that I would soon find interesting work in Paris.

'I lived the early months as a tourist and was soon offered a short-term translating contract at the O.E.C.D., which confirmed my impression that there was no great pressure on me to look ahead. In these early days I only met other O.E.C.D. people, and I took seriously what was expected of me - or perhaps what I felt was expected, since there was in fact no official pressure of any kind. Anyway I thought what was expected of me was to support John in his work by entertaining his colleagues, whether they interested me or not.

'Housing in Paris was cramped even in those days, so we moved to a rather pretty house in Saint-Germain-en-Laye, and I gave up bothering with translating contracts (which were in short supply anyway) to concentrate on decorating the house and tending the huge garden. I considered myself very lucky.

'I tried very hard to be a good international civil servant's wife, to give dinner parties, to go to receptions, to look smart and be interested and informed about John's work. I felt he deserved it; after all I was benefiting every day from his hard work. But the problem was that I discovered I wasn't very good at it. John complained a lot about the way I did things. I've never been a brilliant cook and he would get furious if a dinner party turned out less than perfect. Criticism which he would never have dreamt of levelling at me when we were both working in London, and which I, in any case, would have just shrugged off, became terribly important to me when it concerned what had now become my only creative activity: keeping house for him.

'I started to get anxious about my appearance. I found it difficult to dress in French clothes and at French prices. As for being interested and informed about John's work, I discovered that he didn't value my opinion since I wasn't professionally involved. He liked to tell me about his successes, but not to discuss what it was he was actually doing, or why.

'We grew very far apart in those middle years. John came home less and less early and then less and less often. He had affairs which I, like everybody else, knew about but, like everybody else, pretended I didn't; and I became lonelier and lonelier because I refused to admit what was happening and took great care to keep up appearances.

'A key factor in this was that I still rated John as more important than myself, **because he was working**. I was clearly not a happy and useful wife, and neither was I a happy and useful anything else, and whose fault was it but mine? I had fallen right into the trap of facility, opting for tagging onto John's life, instead of getting on with my own.

'My isolation was reinforced by the stress of being financially dependent on John. Immediately a wife has to ask her husband for pocket money, the relationship between them is fundamentally altered. If, like me, you are too proud to ask often and he tends to forget, you can end up actually worse off than you were before, in spite of his big salary. Why didn't we institute a simple system of

regular payment into my bank account? I didn't want to institution-
alize the pocket-money relationship, but always felt strongly that I
ought at the very least to be responsible for my own personal needs.
Although I am fairly sure that John's stinginess was merely due to
thoughtlessness at the beginning, later on, when we were having
problems, he used it quite deliberately as a weapon.

'I suspect that I am not at all unusual in the total lack of support I had
from my husband in this situation. Things were going so well for him
that he couldn't understand why I had a problem. And he changed:
he became more materialistic, more ambitious, much harder; he
drank too much. He needed a different kind of wife for his social
context. I chose, in the end, not to adjust to his needs.'

It was time, Fiona decided, to embark on a programme of action:
she started psychotherapy - reimbursable on the French social
security system; she began to make friends outside John's sphere
of influence, became involved in a women's group, renewed contact
with her family in Britain whom she had somewhat neglected, and
had a love affair, which helped to restore her battered self-
confidence. Above all she developed activities of her own: at first
this was voluntary work with an organization helping immigrant
children with their schooling. She became very involved with this
and although she was not being paid for it, derived great
satisfaction from the progress she observed in the children and the
contacts she made.

'Eventually I signed up for a **maîtrise** in linguistics at one of the
Paris universities. But I needed something with a more direct
application, so I returned to England for a year to take a Diploma of
Education course. Back in Paris with that, I found a part-time job
lecturing in European history at a private American college, but
unfortunately the college closed down after I had been there a year.
So there I was, back to Square One. Meanwhile my son was born,
John's affairs increased, and loneliness and depression closed in
again.

'Then a group of expatriate women opened up an international playgroup. I offered myself as a voluntary teacher and took my child
along. As he grew older, I was able to leave him there more often. I
took some courses at the university and, as I got to know the staff,
I offered my services there too - unpaid, of course - typing and licking
envelopes.

'After three months one of the secretaries went on maternity leave
and I was asked to replace her temporarily. By the time she came
back, I had made myself indispensable in the running of the department, so instead of being ousted, I was given a half-time post, and,

a year later, when the department expanded, I was put in charge of running the new offshoot full time. I have been there ever since. I earn a living wage and am in a position of responsibility. Three years after I became financially independent, I got a divorce and moved, with my son, into a small flat in the centre of Paris.

'Peter spends many week-ends and part of his holidays with his father. John and I don't meet frequently, but when we do, we're usually on our best behaviour. I don't know whether he intends to stay on in Paris indefinitely. As for myself, I see no reason for going back to Britain. I like Paris, I have made many friends there. I would like to earn a bigger salary - it's not always easy to make ends meet - and if I could find myself a high-powered job in an international city somewhere, I don't think I would object to another move, provided my son came with me and it was on my own terms.'

Despite an outcome which Fiona sees as positive to her own development, the move to Paris cost her a great deal of unhappiness and, in the end, saw the break-up of her marriage. One of the questions she asks herself is whether her relationship with John might have gone in a different direction had they not moved out of London.

'I think that there may have been an incompatibility between us right from the start. If this was the case, it was not at all apparent in London. There, we were shielded by so many things - the fact that I had a profession, and a future, that we were surrounded with friends and family, that we were actively involved in what was going on in Britain at the time - all things that might have taken some of the brunt off marital problems when, and if, they appeared.

'The move to Paris not only put me up against all sorts of difficulties I could not possibly foresee or even understand - isolation, loss of self-confidence, financial dependence, lack of a meaningful occupation - but it also proved to be a kind of catalyst. It showed up problems that must have been there from the start but of which we were quite unaware. It also threw brutal light on our respective weaknesses, but, on the other hand, revealed some strengths.'

MARIANNA

Marianna is German, 41 years old, and a social worker. She lives in Stuttgart with her three children, while her husband Dieter, a corporation executive, commutes from Brussels, where he works.

When Marianna and Dieter married in Stuttgart, in the spring of 1969, Dieter was already working for a large American corporation with a branch in Germany. Marianna, who came from a small town in the Black Forest, was a primary school teacher. She did not particularly care for teaching and had no intention of making a career of it. Soon after her marriage, she decided to give up her job. When Dieter's firm asked them to go to the United States, Marianna was three months pregnant and they decided to wait until the child was born.

Marianna had mixed feelings about that first transfer. She knew, before she married Dieter, that his company had a vigorous transfer policy, and that sooner or later she would have to follow him to another country. Despite the fact that she thought the move ill-timed, and dreaded being in a strange country with a tiny infant, she had no reason to oppose it.

'Besides,' she says, 'I was a very different person then: I was twenty-two years old and in those days and for about ten years after that I believed that men made decisions and women didn't have much say. But I was frightened: I didn't want to have any experiences, didn't want to go on a plane or explore the world. And I didn't even know whether I could cope with a baby.' Dieter thought the experience would be good for both of them. For him, it meant a first important step up the career ladder. That first move, to Minnesota, was as it happened quite a happy one for Marianna, but it was short-lived. After only a few months they were recalled to Germany, where eventually their other two children were born.

Four years later, another transfer came up for Dieter. By this time Marianna had got used to motherhood which she found she enjoyed far more than teaching, but was generally dissatisfied with life in Stuttgart. This was mostly caused by the fact that Dieter's growing status in his firm had led them to move to a rather select suburb in which she felt ill at ease. She therefore welcomed the new transfer as an excuse to move away. 'When I look back on those days,' she says, 'there seems to be a lot of running away from situations that did not feel right.'

They moved to a large town in Pennsylvania, where they lived in the suburbs.

'I was totally lost there. I couldn't identify with my neighbours: they were staunch Catholics and community-spirited and I couldn't stand their racial prejudices. Dieter travelled a lot, sometimes for weeks at a time, so I was often on my own with three small children, no domestic help (I couldn't get any for love or money), stuck in the house and completely isolated.

'I became extremely depressed. I enjoyed being a mother, so I felt guilty about being depressed. I was financially secure and our standard of living was far more comfortable than I had ever known it to be. When he was around, Dieter was loving and helped a lot with the children. I had every reason to be happy. Yet I wasn't. I was depressed and upset without quite knowing why. Now in retrospect I can see the anger building up, but I wasn't aware of it then, and had I been aware of it at any level it would only have added to my guilt and confusion.

'I didn't feel as if I were a whole person, or even a person at all. I was a nothing. I was at everybody's beck and call, someone other people could push around. I didn't particularly want a job - in fact I couldn't think of any job I could do. I doubted my ability to do anything except be a mother and keep house - and that was getting more alienating all the time, although I suppressed any conscious thought of it.

'There was no possibility for anyone to look after the children, so I couldn't go in for any sort of training either. People around me were friendly, but that wasn't enough. They were so different from me that, far from finding their friendliness supportive, I found it suffocating.

'After two years in Pennsylvania, I started to put pressure on Dieter to try and secure a transfer to Brussels. The company had a large branch there, and I'd heard from various people who'd been sent there that it was a good place for expatriates. I thought I'd feel less isolated there. Dieter met with all sorts of difficulties to do with hierarchy and company policy, but eventually he managed to be transferred to Brussels. And I was so pleased, because for the very first time in my life I felt I had had a hand in bringing about a situation that I really wanted.'

Marianna's joy was short-lived. Just as they were about to move into their new house in Brussels, Dieter was told by his managing director that the company was transferring them to Spain.

'This time, I put my foot down. Until that moment I really didn't know I had it in me to refuse outright something that management had decided. I put my foot down, even though I knew that it meant that somehow or other Dieter would be penalized for it - which is in effect what happened. We did stay in Brussels, but we paid for it because Dieter was given no promotion whatsoever for three years. Anyway he was extremely upset by my refusal to budge and kept on bringing it up. But I was adamant. I really felt it would have been wrong for me, and since the children depended on my state of mind for their own well-being, I also felt I was the one who kept the whole thing

going, and that as such I should be given some consideration. So I
believed it was the right decision and I stuck to it.

'I think Dieter was also slightly put out by the fact that suddenly I
had changed from a passive, though moaning, wife to one who could
put her foot down and had even dared put her own well-being before
his career. He didn't know quite how to take this. But despite this
rather stressful beginning, our stay in Brussels was a happy one.
We made a few really good friends for the first time in ages, and
found leisure activities that we could do together and that we both
found stimulating. Also the children were beginning to be more
autonomous and I had more time to myself. For the first time in my
life I felt relaxed and content. I should have known, though, that this
could not last.

'Three years after we got to Belgium, the company decided that
Dieter was again ripe for a move, and they knew perfectly well - just
as I did - that this time if I put my foot down, it might mean the end
of his career. You wouldn't believe the power these people have over
their employees.

'Anyway once more we were transferred to the States - this time to
Atlanta, Georgia. By then I had learnt how demoralizing it could be
to be stuck in a neighbourhood that you did not fit into, so I took my
time to look about and we eventually found a house in a younger and
more liberal kind of suburb. Also, as the children were now all at
school, I spent some time thinking about what I could do with myself.

'The problem was that, despite the fact that my one act of resistance
and my years in Brussels had gone some way towards making me
feel more of a human being, I still lacked self-confidence. Dieter, who
often saw things more clearly than I did, thought that, given my
interests and my earlier training as a teacher, I should start to train
as a social worker. I didn't even have the confidence to think of doing
it without his encouragement and pushing. I felt totally inadequate,
but he kept on saying, "Go on, I know you can do it." So I eventually
got my courage together and applied for a traineeship. And, do you
know, the moment I went for my first training interview, I stopped
doubting myself. It was, quite literally, like turning over a page.

'I finished my two-year training with top grades. I had enjoyed every
minute of it. For the first time I had confidence in my capabilities
beyond those of wife and mother. But, somehow or other, as my self-
confidence increased, I found myself moving further and further
away from Dieter. And again, I began to feel guilty, because he'd
been so supportive. I think - and it's easier to see this in retrospect
- that I had accumulated too much anger and frustration all those

years, and I could only direct this against him. For many years I had been angry at having no control over my life and now I blamed it all on him. For years I lived on a sort of tightrope, not knowing where we'd be sent next, being totally in the company's hands, and I felt as if that insecurity could go on for ever. I couldn't put down roots anywhere: quite literally I knew that I couldn't plant a plum tree and be there long enough to pick the plums.'

Despite the growing rift between Dieter and herself, when the corporation eventually decided to move them back to Stuttgart, Marianna went willingly. She felt that her children needed roots and a cultural identity which they could only really find in their own country.

Back in Stuttgart Marianna found that her American training qualifications were not fully recognized by the German system, and she spent the next year doing a post-graduate course, with some resentment because she found its standard inferior to her American course and because she was chafing at the bit in her desire to find a job. As soon as her year at the university was over, she applied for and was offered a job as a social worker.

She had been working for a year when Dieter's firm decided to send them back to Brussels.

'This time,' she says, 'there was no hesitation, no ambivalence. I just knew I wouldn't go. It was even clearer in my mind than when I refused to follow Dieter to Spain. Now I had a valid reason - which I must admit I didn't completely feel I had at the time of the Spanish transfer. The reason was my career and the validation of my whole life. If anything, I felt it was about time Dieter followed my career for a change. But he wasn't happy about this, and I don't suppose I can really blame him. The company, needless to say, put a lot of pressure on me to give in. They're a paternalistic lot, and they hate to be seen as homebreakers. They felt Dieter needed my support. They never even tried to see my side of it.

'The outcome of all this was that Dieter and I decided that in the end, despite the rifts and conflicts, our marriage was probably strong enough to withstand the strain of commuting. So I stayed in Germany with the children and got on with my career, and Dieter moved to Brussels, where he rented a small apartment, and got on with his. He commutes to Stuttgart every other week-end and we spend all our holidays and long week-ends together in Belgium, Germany or anywhere else.

'It's far from being an ideal solution. You're under a great deal of

strain all the time, and living such different lives has its dangers, but so far it has not been too disastrous. Curiously, I think that this extreme kind of solution has strengthened the bond between us, not because we're less on top of each other, but because I feel more at peace with myself. I feel I have been able to let go of a lot of anger; that I am no longer being controlled by others, but have established my own autonomy. When Dieter and I are together, we're on equal terms. It's almost as if I was in this great big fog for years and years, and suddenly I'm out on the other side and in the sunshine. To say this sounds as if I was never happy during all those years. This isn't true. There were moments when I was moderately happy and content, but perhaps never quite alive, and above all never in control of my own life.'

JULIE

Julie, 46, British, is an artist who makes textile wall-hangings. Her husband, Daniel, is an international computer expert. They have two daughters and now live in Britain.

'I had no idea at all when we got married that we'd be moving around the world. At the time I never realized how much the computing industry relied on the mobility of its experts. For several years before we went abroad we moved within Britain, first from London to the North, then back to London, then to Leicester. We never stayed anywhere longer than two years.

'When our first international move - to Germany - came up, we were rather excited. We thought it was good for the children, who were eight and six at the time. It was just about the time Britain joined the Common Market. We were very much in favour of the idea of Europe, and we thought the children would become little Europeans.

'We all enjoyed Germany. Very few people in the town where we were living spoke any English. The children went to a local school and within three months were speaking German fluently. It took Daniel and me a little longer, but we did end up acquiring reasonably good German. When, after two years, the company decided to move us to the Netherlands we all looked forward to having another similar experience.

'Holland was, if anything, even better. As in Germany, we were in a smallish town, and this one was particularly tranquil and safe. The children, being two years older, were that much more independent and bicycled to school and to their friends' houses. I no longer had to chauffeur them around.

'*It was in Holland that it became clear to us that Dan's work would now entail frequent moves to foreign countries. The idea was not displeasing, but it was obvious that we had to sort out a number of issues if we were going to start living like nomads.*

'*One of these issues had to do with the notion of home and roots. I was very concerned that the children should not feel unstable. Both Dan and I had been brought up with the idea that children had to have a constant base as home, otherwise they might develop problems as they grew up. So we tried to make them understand that "home" was wherever we, as a family, were, and that we must always rely on one another for stability. We could move anywhere as a family, knowing that home was where we were. We hoped that as they grew up, they would feel able to move around freely on their own knowing that they had a firm base in the family unit, rather than in a building or a town that might be labelled "home".*

'*Another issue had to do with me directly. Now that the children were older, at school all day and more autonomous, I felt I had to do something with my life that was more satisfying than vacuuming the house twice a day. I had to find myself an absorbing occupation of some kind and, since we were going to be travelling frequently, I had to be independent of an employer.*'

This was so obviously an important issue that Julie took her time over it. And because she is a methodical and conscientious person, she drew up lists of what her capabilities could lead her to do, of what avenues were closed to her because of circumstances or lack of training, of what her natural inclinations told her to do and of what was most 'portable' among the occupations she came up with.

In Britain she had been to art school and had worked as a craft teacher afterwards. This was a plus to start with she felt, for being a craftsman was one of the few truly portable professions she could think of, one which did not need an employer other than oneself, and one, moreover, in which language problems could be kept to a minimum. Her only reservation about it was that, by its very nature, creative work is solitary work and Julie, despite her self-sufficiency, is extremely gregarious.

Her preference went to pottery, but a potter's material is cumbersome. '*You cannot*', she says, '*carry a kiln in your handbag*'. In the end she settled for work involving textiles, developing, as she went along, a very idiosyncratic style based on a variety of textures, materials and techniques which she used to make large wall-hangings, the idea being that '*if you have a needle and cotton you can do this anywhere, collecting the material from wherever you are*'.

She also firmly announced to her family her intention of having a nine-to-five working day and she insisted that this be respected even though her workshop was in the house. After a family discussion a pattern of household tasks by rota was devised so that Julie's hitherto sole responsibility for house and family maintenance could be lightened and shared.

During her time in the Netherlands Julie worked closely with a group of artists and took part in several group exhibitions. It was important to her to build up her self-confidence by confronting her own work with that of other artists and discussing techniques and theories with them. By the time their next transfer came up, she felt she was ready to work on her own.

This was fortunate for the place Daniel was now moved to was Saudi Arabia, a country that is not an easy one to adjust to for a lot of Western women; some of the restrictions - such as the one forbidding women to drive cars - are crippling. It is a country in which most foreigners live in small, relatively idle cultural enclaves. Julie's profession not only enabled her to survive in an unstimulating expatriate environment, but also gave her the motivation to learn about local textiles and techniques, which became useful to the development of her own work and style. She also enjoyed the constant sunshine, after the gloomy winter months of northern Europe.

When Julie and Daniel went to Saudi Arabia, they sent their daughters off to boarding school in England.

'This was a very unfortunate experience for them. The boarding school they were at was a very Victorian establishment, and quite a shock to them after the rather progressive British school they had been to in the Netherlands. A lot of the members of staff were spinster ladies who'd hidden behind the closed walls of a boarding school because the world was too big a place for them to cope with. And, of course, they were unable to cope with our girls because their experiences were totally beyond their own.

'The girls tried to survive there as best they could for the two years we were in Saudi Arabia, but the elder was beginning to get into trouble - nothing desperate, but she was a constant disturbance in the class. Eventually she got expelled and soon it became quite obvious that the younger would as well. So we withdrew her hastily and we took them with us when we were transferred to Belgium.

'Belgium, I discovered, was a difficult place to sell the kind of work I do. People tend to be rather conservative. Nevertheless I had three

one-person exhibitions and from those I received enough commis-
sions to go on working full time.'

When she was still living in Belgium, Julie came to one of our early
group discussions. As usual, the group was made up of women who
had had very different experiences of international mobility, but
among those who had moved frequently and for short periods of
time, Julie was the only one who was undisturbed by the
phenomenon. *'I've always found moves exciting,'* she said. *'They*
always held an appeal for me. Another country, another life.... I can
never get there fast enough. And, unlike a lot of women who move
frequently, I never write any time off. Most people will tell you that
they have to write off at least six months for each move. Well, not I.
I simply can't afford to. Just think: if you take into account our moves
within Britain, then our moves to Germany, the Netherlands, Saudi
Arabia and Belgium, I reckon I'd have lost three and a half years just
writing off six months every time. That's simply unthinkable.

'No, if my husband's employer said that we must move to Hong Kong
or Timbuctoo at the end of next week - and in this kind of profession
they often don't give you much time to prepare yourself - it wouldn't
worry me in the slightest. I could manage everything that was
necessary in a week and when we'd get there I'd make myself
immediately at home - I feel I've done it so often. I've always wanted
to travel light, but of course one never does. One ends up accumu-
lating the most incredible amount of junk.

'The children love it too, which is a blessing. I don't think I could have
managed if I had children who were not adaptable. Mine always
seem to look forward to the next move. They tend to make friends
fairly easily and maintain contact by letter or telephone.

'The hardest thing I find about moves is leaving friends; but of course
they leave me too. In a mobile society people are on the move all the
time and some people I befriend move away before I do. And I find
it much harder to be left behind than to do the leaving. On the whole,
however, I don't let people get too close. It's a self-preservation
mechanism. We've been in Belgium now though, for three and a half
years, which is the longest we've been anywhere, and this time
there are one or two people whom I shall be devastated to leave. This
time I've been in one place so long that not only have I started to put
in roots, but the roots are coming out of the side of the pot.'

When we next saw Julie, a year and a half later, she was about to
leave Brussels for Britain, where her husband had been transferred
to a permanent post. She admitted to having mixed feelings about
both her impending departure and her attitude to Britain. Five

years in Brussels had reinforced her feeling that she had started to grow roots there and make friendships that she felt strongly about. She found, also that her notion of 'home' was being challenged.

'I have very mixed feelings about going home. I was beginning to think I had got to the point where I had a certain amount of choice. I'm not actually self-supporting, but I could be if I needed to be. I thought, after five years in Brussels, that I was now in a position to say "Yes, I will go", or "No, I won't go this time". But when it actually comes to it I can't do it because there is too strong an emotional bond between my husband and myself.

'He does want to go back to Britain. It takes a decision like this, you know, to crystallize your ideas about home. And although I've always maintained, to make my daughters feel secure, that home was where the family unit is, I don't actually know where home is for myself. I don't feel anywhere is home now. Perhaps this is partly because the family unit is not as whole as it used to be - my elder daughter is at university; and partly because if I really thought I could choose, I might want to stay in Brussels where my friends are very supportive and I feel at ease. We moved so often, too, within Britain, that there is nowhere I can actually call "home" there. I have got family in assorted places but they've all moved away from where we originally came from. Of course there's a sort of familiarity about Britain, about the way things are done there. If I want a doctor, or a hospital or the police, I know how to do it without any hesitation or effort. And the language makes everything so simple. But it doesn't really feel like home.

'I'm a little wary of what I'm going to find when I get there. So many people I know go back to what used to be home and find that they do not slot back in. They're devastated by the realization that not only has life continued while they were away, but that it's changed as well. All the things they were expecting to go back to are not possible any more. They are shocked to find that this longing for home that they've had all those years can never materialize, that it was a false picture of home after all. But of course I haven't got a slot to try and fit back into. Britain is almost like a foreign country to me.

'But in the end, what makes me most wistful about going back is this feeling I cannot get away from - that going back is the return of the wanderer, and that it will be the end of those years of travelling. And because I find the travelling exciting and stimulating, I don't want it to come to an end yet. I don't feel I'm old enough to settle down and grow radishes.

'I force myself to look at the positive aspects, and, to be honest, there are several. We've never owned any property anywhere, and both Dan and I have just become aware of how important this notion of having your own place is. Then there's the aspects that relate to my work. I have a feeling that London will be more open to an unusual style such as the one I've developed and that the market will be much bigger. Of course the competition will be much higher, but I look forward to the stimulation of finding out what other people are doing.

'One of the most important things, however, about that return to Britain is that we shall be near my elder daughter again. She's at university there now and is not finding it easy. Both my girls started travelling by themselves at quite an early age and I find them very mature. I felt that Anne was totally capable of looking after herself in an environment outside her home. But as it happens, she suffered greatly from not having a support system such as the family within easy reach. I think perhaps, when I tried to make them feel secure by putting emphasis on the family unit, I was too emphatic about it. I should have given her more independence from the family as well.

'But all will be well in the end. I'm an eternal optimist in that when something is going to happen, I tend to gear myself to see the positive side. It's true that with this move I'm more ambivalent. Basically, as I said, it's perhaps because I feel at the moment that it's going to be the end of those wonderful trips around the world, the end of a long period of change and stimulating experience. I can't get away from that thought and therefore this impending move is not as exciting as any of the others. But I keep on telling myself that all will be well.'

II

START OF A JOURNEY

Fiona, Marianna, Julie. Three different stories; three different women,
with one thing in common - all three followed their husbands abroad
for reasons connected with his work.

If we chose to put these stories as a preamble to this book, it is not
because we think that each of them is particularly representative
of an expatriate situation. (There is no such thing as a characteristic expatriate situation, or even characteristic expatriate situations, despite the fact that some elements will be common to all
of them. Each varies according to the individuals and circumstances that compound it.) We chose them rather because within
them altogether can be found the issues and themes that ran like
many threads through the testimonies we gathered from over three
hundred expatriate wives during the four years it took us to collect,
analyze and present the material of this book.

These issues and themes that make up the fabric of our study are
a mixture of the positive and the negative, of plain facts and
individual reactions, of rationally worked-out strategies and overwhelming emotions. Many are heavy with ambivalence and the
boundaries between them often blurred. Some are true of mobility
in general; some apply to one particular type of mobility rather than
another. Others apply to a certain category of women rather than
another. Many are contested and controversial.

Here, pell-mell, are some of the themes that were voiced by the
women who took part in this study and are reflected in one or
another of the three stories presented as a preamble: the disruption
and uncertainty caused by transplantation to another country; the
difficulty of preserving some form of continuity in one's life; the
stimulation of going to live in a foreign land, of coming face to face
with another culture, of meeting new challenges; the very real,
though often understated appeal of a financially more comfortable
lifestyle than one might have in one's own country; loneliness and
culture-shock; the frustration of being unable to find a stimulating
job or occupation of one's own; anger at having put oneself in the
position of being a camp-follower; guilt at feeling angry, especially
if all outward signs point to a life of greater material comfort and
higher social status; the opportunity to travel extensively, given by
both a higher standard of living and a new environment; frustration
at being temporarily rendered speechless and helpless through
language difficulties.

Similar contradictions operate on another level. Among the deeper
repercussions of mobility are: changes in the pattern of relationships within the couple and family and the need to reassess these;
the burden of being financially dependent on one's husband,

which is all the greater if one has known financial autonomy in the past; the loss of one's familiar support structures; the difficulty of making new friendships in a transient society; the loss of self-confidence through the interruption of a professional activity; the challenge of finding employment abroad which may lead one to acquire additional training, to consider other avenues or to invent or devise for oneself some form of 'portable' profession; the feeling of being an alien both in one's host country and in one's own country; the fear of what transience and rootlessness might do to one's children; the need to reassess one's notion of roots, home and identity. Full of contradictions and ambiguity, the situation of expatriate wives can only reinforce the feelings of confusion and helplessness that beset many women, especially in the early months of a move abroad.

Fiona's, Marianna's and Julie's stories will strike many chords in other expatriate women. Each of them, in its own way, strikes chords in us, the authors of this book; not simply because they express the questions, fears, hopes, complaints, rejoicings we heard during our research, but also, and perhaps mostly, because our motivation to write a book about expatriate wives came originally from a reflection upon our own circumstances and feelings in which echoes of these stories can be found.

As expatriate wives ourselves we sensed that our situation was fraught with ambivalence and contradictions and that the way we coped with it fluctuated according to circumstances, time, experiences, moods and the few conversations we had about it with other women like us. In other words we felt that it was a situation which was unclear and the source of a certain confusion and insecurity, perhaps because we had not explored sufficiently some of its facets and the implications it held for us and for what we expected from our lives.

The more we reflected upon it, the more we discussed the problems confronting us and those of our friends who were also expatriates, the more we became aware that many of our experiences and feelings were shared by a lot of other women around us. At the same time we perceived in several of these women a reluctance, with overtones of guilt, to talk about this openly. It was almost as if peering at the underside of the expatriate situation were taboo, as if these women themselves were conniving at keeping their situation confused. This was thrown into greater emphasis by the relief other women expressed at not being alone in their inability to cope successfully with a difficult situation, and served to confirm our perception that the situation in question was one that was not only confused and confusing but contradictory and controversial. As so often happens once you have started to focus on a specific situation, you become very alert to anything that is relevant to it. We started to read about it with increasing frequency in newspapers and magazines. Very soon it became obvious to us that we had not been seeing the wood for the trees: by keeping our attention focussed on our own situation and that of the women around us, we had not realized that that very situation was an extremely widespread by-product of international mobility; that it was, in fact, a social phenomenon, and one that created problems which radiated well beyond those of the women themselves.

A mere glance at some of the headlines we collected gives an idea of the extent and virulence of the phenomenon, though they all tend to favour the more negative aspects of expatriate life: 'The high cost of a moving experience'.... 'Romance of work abroad can turn into depression and break-up of family'.... 'High-flyer's return can be thud'.... 'Mobility versus marriage....' [1]

'The stress of living and working abroad destroys marriages,' reported an article in *The Times*, 'causes mental breakdowns in both men and women, and can lead to *anorexia nervosa* in their children.... Romantic notions of an exciting life, more money, servants and an instant circle of friends are often crushed by depression, anxiety, isolation and unhappiness.' [2]

Another article, entitled 'Flagging round the Flag', [3] quoted a British Council spokesman who admitted that mobility was one of the major causes of the rising number of divorces and mental and nervous breakdowns among the staff of the British Council and the British Diplomatic Service. Furthermore, applications to enter these organizations were falling because of the geographical mobility involved.

Certain articles in the European and American press were particularly concerned with the wives of members of the armed forces and the 'oppressive, claustrophobic and anachronistic life led by women who have no status other than that conferred on them by their husband's rank'.[4] An increasing number of wives reportedly refused to accompany their husbands on their incessant moves, and among those who did, more and more were taking to drink as an escape from their unhappiness. This was corroborated by a study of military wives which we read later, and which revealed a devastatingly high percentage - 90% - of self-reported drinkers among the wives of armed forces personnel. [5]

'An American survey', declared an article in *The Economist*, 'suggests that as many as one in three American expatriates fails to complete the full tour of duty abroad. European companies with perhaps only a one-in-seven failure rate, are said to do rather better.' [6]

The same article reported that, as a result of being posted abroad, there were often several expatriates at any one time recovering from nervous breakdowns at the Charter Clinic in London, a subsidiary of the American Charter Medical Corporation of Georgia.

'The list of patients makes dismal reading. They include spouses suffering from withdrawal, severe depressives, alcoholics created by loneliness and boredom, suicidal teenagers.' [7]

So significant was the failure rate among expatriates, and so expensive for the companies repatriating them, that various studies, sponsored by employers, were conducted among expatriate families. The Dutch electronics company Philips worked with a psychologist at the Institute for Research on Intercultural Cooperation, as did several other Dutch, British and Swedish firms. In London, two psychiatrists, Dr Richard Caplan of St George's Hospital and Dr Maurice Lipsedge of Guy's Hospital, monitored a research project on fifty couples posted overseas by companies and governments.

It was clear, from a conversation we had with Dr Lipsedge, that many of the nervous breakdowns among the expatriates he was treating were brought about or precipitated by external factors, such as stress resulting from the working and living conditions in politically unstable countries or in areas in which the climate and culture are particularly difficult for Westerners to adjust to. Over and above this, however, the situation in which the repatriation and therapeutic treatment of expatriate families became necessary, was encouraged by inadequate conditions of candidate selection and preparation on the part of the employers, as well as failure to take into account some of the difficulties confronting wives. This tallied perfectly with the information we ourselves had obtained from many of the expatriate women with whom we had discussed the subject.

As we started to hunt around for more detailed material on expatriates, we realized that, curiously, despite the growing concern on the part of employers and the interest of newspapers, very little had been written on the subject. There were a number of reports that few people knew about and fewer still could consult and a couple of books which had been published in very small runs in Switzerland and France. [8] The sample of women these books were based on was also small and specific: one dealt with 'oecumenical wives' in Geneva and the other with French wives in Venezuela. Like our own study, these had been researched and written by expatriate wives, and here too, it was interesting that the problems they raised were similar to those we ourselves had become aware of.

The dearth of readily available studies on the subject and our own strong interest thus encouraged us to embark on a project which, we hoped, might give a general picture of the situation of expatriate wives, encourage greater awareness of their problems, be of use to their husbands' employers and, above all, raise questions. We also hoped that, through the experiences and testimonies of the women in our study, other women might find answers to their own questions, or at least solace in the fact that they were not alone.

With the collaboration of a small number of friends who were interested in the project - but whose circumstances eventually forced them, to our great regret, to drop out of it - we decided to limit the study to the situation within Europe of women of different nationalities who had moved abroad for reasons directly connected with their husbands' professions. We felt that extending the geographical framework to other continents would bring in a number of very different circumstantial problems than were to be found in Europe. Similarly we originally planned to include, as an appendix, a smaller, comparative study of men who had followed their wives abroad for the same reasons, but we came across too few men in that position to be able to gather sufficient data on this interesting reversal of roles.

Brussels was ideal as the centre of our research project, not only because we were living there and had easy access to a large number of expatriates, but also because, by virtue of its role as the capital of Europe, it is one of the most truly international small cities in the world, a virtually obligatory stop for many diplomats, journalists or corporate gipsies, a *forum romanum* for expatriates, as one woman called it. Many of the women we met there had spent years in other countries and could talk about their different experiences. Besides, we had friends and acquaintances in other European countries who were willing to help with our research, so the sample on which we worked was eventually extended well beyond Brussels.

The research consisted of devising, distributing and recovering a twelve-page questionnaire (these questionnaires were distributed in their hundreds in Belgium, France, Britain, the Netherlands, the Scandinavian countries, Germany, Switzerland, Italy, Spain, Portugal and Greece; over 300 of them were laboriously filled in and sent back to us), and setting up individual interviews and group discussions, in Brussels and other cities in Europe. Articles in *The Bulletin*, the chief English-language weekly in Belgium, and, later

in its German equivalent, *Der Kontakt*, presented and discussed the project and invited women who were interested in giving their testimonies or learning more about it to get in touch with us.
The result of this was, apart from the 300-odd questionnaires, hundreds of hours of taped interviews and group discussions made over a period of two years. After that came the long task of sorting out the material and writing the text.

The questionnaires provided both quantitative and qualitative data - some of which is discussed in Part IV of the book, *Moving Figures in a Moving Landscape* - and gave us a sample that was representative not only of every area of expatriate life but also of every kind of attitude on the part of the women themselves. Among these women were many who expressed mostly satisfaction with their situation and their testimonies and the data they provided must be taken as an indication that everything in international mobility is not stamped with ambiguity, frustration and difficulty.

If, however, our sample had consisted only of positive, or mostly positive, testimonies, we would not have had a book to write. So, despite the fact that this sample is representative of expatriate wives in general, our study itself may be said to rely more heavily on the testimonies of women who were feeling less clearly contented about their situation, who questioned many aspects of it, who tried to find answers and who, often, looked beyond it to wider issues. These are mostly women who, having filled in their questionnaires or read about our project, contacted us directly and expressed the wish to talk to us about themselves. It is they who provide the *raison d'être* of this book.

Originally we intended to present our findings as they are usually set up in sociological studies, but, interesting as the analyses and results were to us, we were aware that in the process of sorting them out and dissecting them, the life and spontaneity that had pervaded every aspect of our dealings with hundreds of expatriate wives were lost.

We therefore resolved to try and convey a little of that immediacy and spontaneity by presenting some of the main issues in our study in the form of group discussions, consisting on average of five or six women, excluding ourselves, and centered around themes such as international mobility in general, family relationships, women's professional activities and the prospect of home - subjects that sometimes slightly overlap or merge into one another as discussions unfold.

In choosing to present some of our material in this thematic way we have had to edit some of our taped discussions and interviews, to make a patchwork of them, as it were, lifting material here and there and placing it in a different context to emphasize a point or introduce a new point. We hope that the women who will recognize their own voices will forgive us for taking this necessary liberty and we feel confident that in doing so we did not in any way betray the essence of what each of them had to say.

In the last part of the book, which is an overview, we have tried to place the situation of expatriate wives in its social and historical context, gather together some of the strands that weave in and out of the group discussions, giving them substance and flavour, and examine them against the wider background of our study.

Throughout the book we have tried to protect the identity of the women by changing their names and their husbands' and, where they were too recognizable and had expressed the wish to remain unidentified, we have changed their nationality and other biographical or circumstantial details. Here again, the substance of what women told us, and the impact of their personalities and experiences remain unchanged. Their voices are still their own.

[1]. Respectively, *The Sunday Times*, 11 March 1984; *The Times*, 12 April 1985; *The Sunday Times*, 20 April 1986; *The Guardian*, 5 June 1985.
[2]. *The Times*, 12 April 1985.
[3]. *The Times*, 10 June 1983.
[4]. *The Sunday Times*, 3 February 1983.
[5]. Garrett, G. R. *et al*, 'Drinking and the Military Wife: A Study of Married Women in Overseas Base Communities', in Hunter, E. G. and Nice, D. S. (eds), *Military Families: Adaptation to Change*, New York, 1978.
[6]. *The Economist*, 3 March 1984.
[7]. Ibid
[8]. Geneva Women's Cooperative, *With Our Consent?*, Geneva 1983; and Peskine, Brigitte, and Abergel, Micheline, *Femmes expatriées*, Paris, 1982.

III

VOICES IN THE EVENING

1

Out into the Blue

They sailed away for a year and a day,
To the land where the Bong-tree grows.

Edward Lear,
The Owl and the Pussycat, London, 1871

The discussion that follows took place in Brussels in October 1985. The women present that evening were Abby, 52, American; Emma, 46, British; Lena, 36, American; Isabelle, 53, Belgian; Amanda, 51, American; and the two authors of this book*.

EG-

As you know, we're here tonight to talk about a condition that's common to all of us - apart from the fact that we're women - which is that we are all living out of our own countries, and that we came to live abroad because of our husbands' careers.

'As a social species we're actually beginning to make headlines, although these tend to show the more negative aspects of living abroad. We've been described by various writers as "trailing spouses" or "camp-followers". Together with our husbands and children we are part of a new breed: the "new nomads". People think of us as latter-day memsahibs, with all that this term may evoke. And with the growth of international mobility and the prospect of 1992**, which most of us who are living in Brussels cannot avoid being aware of, it's very likely that the future will produce many more women in our situation.

'We know, from the questionnaires you filled in, that four of you have extensive experience of international mobility, and that one of you - Lena - is here on what we call a "one-off" stay abroad. Morwenna and I, on the other hand, are here for an indefinite period of time. So, between the seven of us we cover the three main types of international moves: the "one-off", usually fairly short move; the frequent, shortish type of move commonly associated with diplomatic life, business transfers and international experts; and the lengthier open-ended or indefinite move which certain international civil servants like the E.C. fonctionnaires are called upon to make.

'We'd like to start this discussion by asking each one of you in turn to tell us briefly who you are, what your experience of international mobility has been until now and what you feel about it. And then we'll take up the various themes as they develop. Who shall we start with?

Abby -

I don't mind beginning the discussion. I certainly have enough to talk about since my relocation experience is quite a long one. My name's Abby, I'm an American, 52 years old. My husband's an international accountant and we have three grown-up children who are all in the States. We'd already moved several times within the States before coming to Europe: from New York to the back-

---

* Hereafter referred to by their initials EG and MJ.

**The date by which barriers to free movement within the E.C. of goods, services, capital and persons must be removed.

woods of the West, from Arizona to California. Every time we moved
I changed jobs: I went from being a medical secretary to working
in computers, and then in California I went into high fashion,
which was really fun. Then my husband, who's German, was
moved to the Vienna office of his company and there I got involved
with the Good Friends - like the Samaritans in the States - doing
P.R. work. After a few years we were sent to Brussels, and here I
started to do a lot of voluntary work with the Parents-Teachers
Association at the International School. I eventually got a paid job
with the psychologist there; the salary wasn't much, but it was
important to me just to get paid. At the same time I got involved with
a British friend who'd started an English-language radio channel
in Brussels - something I'd never done before. So now I'm pushing
buttons on the radio show, interviewing people, putting up ideas
for shows, and finding it all fascinating.

MJ -
You sound as if you enjoy moving.

Abby -
Oh, I think mobility's fantastic if you open yourself up to it. And to
do that, you've got to be flexible. I've enjoyed all my moves, both
here in Europe and in the States. I've met people I'd never have met
and done things I'd never have done if I had remained in New York
City. But now it looks as though another move is on the horizon -
back to the States - and I'm not feeling so great about this one. But
I'll tell you about that later.

MJ -
Right. What about you, Emma, you've moved about a lot, haven't
you?

Emma -
We certainly have as my husband's in the British Diplomatic
Service. I'm 46, we have two teenage daughters, we've been in
Brussels two years and we're about to move to Paris. We've been
on the move since 1965: first to Finland for three months, then
Hungary for two years, Geneva for one year, the Cameroons for two
years, Brussels, and soon Paris. And of course, in between we had
a few home leaves.

MJ -
Do you enjoy moving?

Emma -
Yes, but I'm getting a bit weary. I liked Moscow best, I think. We
travelled a lot in Russia, and it was very interesting. I loved the

language, the people, the history, everything about it really. But then I've loved everywhere I've been. When you think back, each place has a distinctive flavour, like each person you've known.

'The first six months are always dreadful. I write off the first six months anywhere. But what I find now, as I get older, is that I'm resenting all these wasted first six months. I'm objecting to the amount of my life that is taken up by the process of moving, meeting new people, settling in, readjusting and starting my life all over again. This is one area in which experience doesn't help. There are some things you can't bypass: you can't make friends instantaneously; you can't settle down into a place instantaneously.

EG -
Isabelle, what about you?

Isabelle -
I am 53, Belgian, and a lawyer by profession. My husband works for the World Bank and we have three teenage children. Our life as nomads started on the very day of our wedding. We spent two years in England, then came back to Belgium for two years. Then there were two years in the States, another two years back in Belgium, then eight years in Paris. By that time my husband was spending two out of these eight years travelling backwards and forwards to the Congo. Later, he was sent back to Brussels, but I stayed in Paris with the children, because of my job - I was working for an NGO.* Eventually, when I joined him in Brussels, on the very day I hung the curtains in our new house, he said he was being sent to Washington. I decided to remain in Belgium. It was only going to be for two years, but it has been going on for twelve years now - a kind of commuting marriage between Washington and Brussels.

EG -
And how do you feel about that?

Isabelle -
It's complicated. We've travelled together a great deal all around the world and that is fun. We often try to meet in places other than Brussels or Washington - we just met in India, and that was like a holiday. Once - when I was living in Paris and working for the NGO and he was in Africa a lot - we met in Dakar. I remember we were sitting at a table in a restaurant and at some point we both took out our diaries to have a look at our schedules and decide where in the world we were going to meet next. And suddenly we realized that the people at the next table were listening to our conversation and it was obvious they thought we were having an

*Non-Governmental Organisation

affair. We were having great fun at that period in our lives.

'But our present set-up, of course, means that we no longer share an everyday life together. These meetings are like a holiday and yet not like a holiday because you may have accumulated all sorts of problems in the meantime that you have to discuss, and sometimes these problems are not easy to explain to someone who's been leading a totally different life. We don't get bored or fed up because we don't see each other often enough, and when we meet it's a special occasion for the whole family. I realized the other day that the children had got all dressed up for a family dinner because he was there and they felt it was a special occasion. But I think it's been extremely hard for him, harder than I had realized. He's been more alone in Washington than I've been here. I have the family to care for.

EG -
Lena, your experience must be quite different. This is, I believe, your first move abroad and you'll be going home to the United States when your husband's posting comes to an end.

Lena -
Yes, we've been here two and a half years and are going back to the States in the spring. I'm 36 years old, I was born in New York City and my husband's working for N.A.T.O.

MJ -
Have you been working in Brussels?

Lena -
I've been doing some freelance corporate fund-raising for a music association here. My experience of mobility is practically non-existent, except that I moved from New York to Washington about ten years ago.

'I started off teaching the piano in the States, then I got into art management and started a chamber music series in Washington. I did it alone for the first year, and continued teaching the piano to make money, then a good friend joined me and we did it together. It was our fifth season when my husband was suddenly posted to Brussels.

'I actually was getting sick of fund-raising and I thought it would be wonderful to move to Brussels. I told myself: "I'll read, I'll do this, I'll do that...." My husband has a strong streak of wanderlust and he'd turned down other things for me, so I made the decision to follow him willingly.

'When we got here, however, after the first six weeks which were lovely, I found it extremely difficult. I was utterly frustrated because I had nothing to do - I didn't have any children at that point. I had come from working over forty hours a week at something that I enjoyed doing to doing nothing at all, so I really had a hard time.

'Then after a few months I saw an ad in *The Bulletin* about corporate fund raising for a music organization. I called up the director and I've been working at it ever since. It's freelance work so I have to do it from my house mostly, which I don't like - it's too isolated for me. And I have to be so disciplined.... Still, it's better than nothing.

'It wasn't until last April, when my son was born, that I started to like it here. I'm not used to moving. I don't like it. I know it's good for me, but I don't like it.

EG -
Why do you think it's good for you?

Lena -
I suppose it defines time in a way. We've been here two and a half years. I see it as a chunk in my life. Or out of my life, perhaps. Also it did cause me to work on my French. But these are not my goals: they are not the things that are really important to me. My interests are in creating something and keeping it going, developing intimate friendships and keeping them. And I find that very hard here.

'Before our son was born, I couldn't structure my own day. I didn't know what to do with myself. I was going crazy. All these things I thought I'd do when I got to Europe, I wasn't interested in doing them when I was right upon them. I think it's deadly to stay in your house no matter how great your house is. I found myself turning into a little groundhog, and yet the effort to get out - even to get out of bed - was enormous.

EG -
This sort of apathy came over me too when I first came to Brussels. In London, where I'd worked in publishing, and later in Paris, where I was doing all sorts of things, I never used to wear a watch. Even with appointments, business lunches and office life I never felt the need to check what the time was.

'When I came here, after the first frantic few weeks, things got back to a "normal" rhythm. Only to me it was completely abnormal. The only imperative I had was to go and get my son from school at 4 p.m. and have supper ready for 7.30. Otherwise the day was my own. I hardly knew anybody, my husband was too busy settling into his new job to meet me for lunch. I could have spent the entire day in bed and no one would have been the wiser. Then I found myself wearing an old watch of my husband's and, after a while, I couldn't take it off without feeling totally lost. I suppose it was a way of making myself so aware of time that I was compelled to try and structure it.

MJ -
Amanda, I believe that even as a child you moved around a lot because your parents were in the Foreign Service. And now you are still moving.

Amanda -
Yes, and I travelled all over the Far East when I was a child. I'm a Foreign Service wife too, only I don't really feel like one, because I met my husband when he'd already been in the Service a while, and I'd become an actress, living in California. So I still feel a bit of an outsider.

'We've moved about six times, for periods of four, six, three, another three, one and two years. One never knows how long it's going to be - it could be extended, or it could suddenly be cut short. I've never been able to get moving down to a fine art. I expect some people do. Every time it's different: there are some places you're happy to move to and some places you dread. And this colours your whole move.

'Our first move was to Paris and I was thrilled. I was terribly excited. At the time I was acting in a play I hadn't wanted to do and Paris offered a way out. Also I'd never been to Europe, so I was very pleased.

'I'm one of those women who almost enjoy, in a masochistic way, the actual process of moving. Husbands usually leave before the rest of the family - that's a classic thing - and the packing and moving and renting and painting is all done by the women with a certain amount of self-satisfaction. It's just a wonderful opportunity to grouse. You can go full blast, moaning away, yet with a certain sense of accomplishment because you've managed to survive on your own.

MJ -
I'd like to ask those of you who are perpetual movers whether there are any strategies that one can develop to make the process easier for all concerned?

Isabelle -

Our strategy was always to settle down immediately as if every move was to be permanent. This doesn't mean that there were curtains everywhere. It's more a question of what goes on in your mind - it's your attitude. We always unpacked everything very quickly and organized our lives as if we were going to be there for a long time. That is very important, and I understood it in Washington, where we had British friends who had already been there for two years before we got there. They told us that their daughter, who was three and a half, was homesick for England. And I said, "My Lord, how can that tiny child be homesick for a home she's hardly known?" I think this was due more to her parents' attitude, and we decided there and then that we would never cultivate that sort of nostalgia.... Of course, as a result, we don't feel attached anywhere.

Amanda -

I agree with you. I've heard it said, and I've lived it, and I know it to be true that you can't live with nostalgia. It's just too dangerous. It's difficult, though, to convince yourself that you're going to be someplace for a long time when you know you're not. When you have a garden, for instance, you have to go out and plant things as if you're going to be there for twenty years. And the same attitude's valid for a house, for everything. The people I have known to have been happiest are those who have not lived with one suitcase always open under the bed, ready to go. You definitely have to make a psychological commitment when you arrive on a new posting. I believe in giving the place every chance.

MJ -

Yes. I did quite the opposite when I first arrived in Belgium, and I realize now how wrong it was. I thought it was only going to be for two years, though it was an open-ended contract, and I didn't put any effort into the house that we had rented. There were unpacked boxes in the basement and I didn't hang all the pictures. I didn't think it was worthwhile spending any money on carpets, so there was only lino. It always seemed desolate and not a bit like home. That's something I'd never do again, even if I knew for certain that we'd be up and off in a short time.

Emma -

If there's one very practical tip I might give anybody it is that they should try to take along with them on the plane to a new country a few things that would normally travel with the rest of the luggage but that might make their life easier those first few days. One of the things I hate most is arriving in a new kitchen that's usually underequipped, so my Magimix always travels with me on the plane. And I must have the most well-travelled spice jars in the world. You have the right to say you must have certain things with you on the plane - it may just be half-a-dozen miscellaneous things, but they'll make you feel less of an alien when you arrive.

Amanda -
Yes, and if you have children, it is terribly important to take their favourite toys with you. I've travelled on planes with old teddy bears, bits of wallpaper, silly things like that. I think you have to do that - it's your nest you're taking with you. You have to cushion the blow as much as you can.

Isabelle -
I feel exactly like you. The first time we moved with the children, I made a big mistake. I saw the move as an opportunity to clear out my children's toys, and I realized that was absolutely wrong. Small children want their tiny world with them and you should keep all their belongings with you and move them every time you move and unpack them all. You might throw away a few things later, but when they arrive in a new place they must have with them their old teddy-bears and one-armed dolls.

Abby -
It's not only the children that need cushioning, it's us adults too! Early days anywhere are hell for anyone. I can tell you, my first days in Vienna were pretty harrowing, though it just seems funny now.

'Half an hour after the removal van arrived with all our furniture, we had the police at the door. The next-door neighbour had called them because the truck was hanging an eighth of a centimetre over the driveway of his house. He actually even came out with a tape measure and a polaroid camera, took pictures and then measured the distance from his driveway to the truck.

'The next day I had workmen hooking up the washing-machine and the refrigerator we had brought over from the States. We had a huge transformer for them. When my husband left for work that morning, he said: "Make sure they don't cut the plug off when they hook up the refrigerator." I said: "How do you say that in German?", but in his rush he forgot to tell me, so that I had to fumble with my dictionary and phrase book, and, by the time I'd come to the phrase I wanted, the plug had been cut. This was just one of many tiny things that got me mad with frustration at first. They make you feel so dumb!

Lena -
I felt a real dummy too at first. I remember going to the doctor when

I first arrived. I had a slight gynaecological problem, so I went to see a specialist. He didn't speak English and I only had schoolgirl French. But anyway he gave me a prescription and I got the medicine from the pharmacy. Ten days later, however, I still had the problem. So I went back to the doctor and he was very puzzled that the medicine had not worked. He said - in French: "I don't understand. What have you been doing with these? Where have you been putting them?" It turned out, of course, that he'd given me antibiotic suppositories and I'd been using them as vaginal pessaries!

MJ -
I interviewed a Japanese woman the other day, and she told me that when she first arrived in Brussels from Tokyo, her husband's predecessor's wife told her that Brussels tap water was not fit for drinking. What she probably meant was that the water was hard and didn't taste terribly nice. But poor Kimi thought that it was infested with germs and for the next three months, until somebody else enlightened her, she proceeded to wash everything except clothes in mineral water out of bottles!

EG -
But you know, it isn't just language problems that make first days harrowing. I think it's the state of mind one's in. One feels cut off from reality to some extent. We came over from France, so there was no language problem. At the beginning the telephone had not yet been put in and our car suddenly packed up. The very night the car collapsed, our little boy, who was three at the time, woke up at two o'clock in the morning with a horrible sort of barking cough. He had a very high temperature and was choking. It was very dramatic. We were quite beside ourselves with worry - in fact we were so beside ourselves in every way that, instead of knocking on the neighbours' door, which anybody in their right mind would have done, my husband made for the nearest public telephone, which was a good quarter of a mile away. When he got there, however, he found that hooligans had ripped the phone out. So off he went in search of another one. By the time the doctor arrived, it was nearly 6 a.m. Our boy turned out to have acute laryngitis, made worse by the central heating and his condition was not serious. But what a night! What has stayed with me was how completely helpless we both were in this new environment.

MJ -
Think of how much more helpless you might have been if you didn't speak any French. Not being able to speak the language makes you feel so solitary, as well. I remember a friend whose husband is a journalist telling me how, as soon as they had arrived in Paris, her

husband had been sent off on an assignment for several days. Dip, my friend, is a very shy person, but she became so desperate for human contact after a few days that she stopped someone in the market whom she overheard speaking English and started to talk to him frantically, just to be able to have some contact.

Emma -
I must admit that we're very cushioned from this sort of experience in the diplomatic service. We not only get all sorts of information from the people on the spot, but when you arrive there is already an existing infrastructure and a social network. You get the feeling that you arrive in a group that's already formed and into which you're immediately integrated.

Isabelle -
You are lucky in some ways to have that immediate resource. But don't you think that the greatest mistake we all make is to expect other people to look after us when we arrive? I think this is nonsense: you are the *demandeur,* and so *you* have to do the running. If you feel isolated, you must seek people out. If you meet someone you like, you have to say right away: "I'd like to meet you again. Can we have lunch?" It isn't easy, and it puts you at risk - people may refuse you - but I think it's the right attitude.

Lena -
But how self-confident you must be to do that! And the problem is that, when you first arrive somewhere completely unfamiliar, you lose your self-confidence. You lose your normal reactions, as Enid was saying a few minutes ago. In some ways, I think, you lose your identity. You're only here because of your husband and no one knows who you are. Even your status may conspire against you! Let me tell you what happened to me.

Two weeks after we moved here, I made a phone call to the N.A.T.O. support group and they said: "What's your status?" I said: "What do you mean?" The woman said: "Are you a dependent wife?" I said: "Let me think about this for a minute." She said: "No, no, no. Are you here because your husband is working?" I said: "Well, yes." And she said; "O.K., then you're a D.W. - Dependent Wife. That's your status. When you go to the clinic, for instance, you'll have to give your status. D.W. That's you." I was completely shocked. You're a D.W. because you're husband's got a job with the government. Even if you're stinking rich or are employed yourself, your status remains that of a Dependent Wife. It doesn't matter what or who you are, you're branded. And what's really frightening is that I don't even think about it any more. I've accepted it.

EG -
There is a general feeling of floundering, isn't there, at the beginning, when no one knows who you really are and you have no structure to fall back on. There's a big difference between a husband who moves from one work structure to another and a wife who's got to rebuild her own support structure every time. A lot of people talk about culture shock, but I think there is also, and above all, an inner culture shock which comes from this stripping of everything one is familiar with.

Emma -
You know, even diplomatic wives who come into a ready-made support structure have this awful period of adjustment, this inner culture shock, as you say. And there's indeed a huge difference between a husband's experience in a move and a wife's.

'When all's said and done, my husband doesn't have that much adapting to do. He moves from one familiar structure to another. There are sometimes familiar faces, people he's known from the past, who will be working with him. He moves from one office to another office; people seem delighted to see him. He has lunch with this person, coffee with that person, and a definite job to do, there on his desk, in front of him. All right, he can choose which direction he'll take his job or his life, how much emphasis he'll put on meeting this or that sort of people, but he won't have this total floundering that I have every time I get to a new place. It's not just a question of support structure, it's a perpetual reviewing of who and what you are: whether to make something of your life, whether to waste your time at coffee mornings, whether to go and be a lady bountiful, whether to learn a new skill - it's your whole personality that's put in jeopardy every time you move.

MJ -
But the women too have a definite job to do, at least at the beginning, and that is to settle the family in. I think that the really painful period of adjustment often comes later, when everyone has been settled in and the wife finds herself with more time on her hands. In a sense, the women who may suffer most immediately from this floundering feeling are those who don't have children to settle in.

Lena -
I agree with you here. If I had had my son when we first arrived, he might have provided the structure I needed, and I would not have had so much time to dwell on my own little miseries because I would have had to make sure that he was alright.

MJ -
Having a list of definite things to do might help.

Lena -
It didn't help me. I had all sorts of things I wanted to do and didn't do any of them - at least not then.

MJ -
Nevertheless there are usually priorities that have to be attended to, after you've got a roof over your head - which is often something that people have settled even before they arrive. What are the priorities? Let's have a quick list.

Amanda -
Children, of course, if you have any. The most important thing is to get them into a good school and into a routine - in terms of timetables, meals, routes, shopping, sports, treats and so on. Once the routine is established, if they're over a certain age, they'll probably look after themselves.

Isabelle -
An important priority is to find your way around as soon as possible. And people you are going to need: doctors, pediatricians, dentists, plumbers, etc. And getting organized about the language.

Abby -
The language is most important. You've got to learn the language of the country you're in. If you go to a country where you don't speak the language, that's the toughest, but that's the best, because it forces you to learn it.

Lena -
I felt like a five-year-old when I arrived and I was faced with a language I could hardly understand. I'd taken French at school in the States, but what little I thought I remembered was no use to me at all. You're totally cut off not only from understanding other people but from expressing yourself, your pleasure, your anger, anything. And people speak to you as if you're a simpleton. They mouth their words exaggeratedly and mime things. I thought I'd die with frustration at first.

Emma -
Yes, but if you're someone who's constantly being shipped from pillar to post, you may decide that it isn't worth getting to know the language, because by the time you feel you've got somewhere with it, lo and behold, you're packing your cases again, and you're off to a new place with a new language. And if you allow yourself to get

discouraged, if you're not careful, you start thinking: "Well, what's the point of doing it all over again?"

'A lot of women have said this to me about languages, because I took a lot of trouble to learn Hungarian and, later, to learn Russian. And people said: "Oh, when you're older, you won't bother. You can't keep on doing it." And I thought that was dreadful and one should keep on doing it. But now I see you can get to the point of thinking: "It's only for three years, so what's the point?"

Amanda -
Yes, that's one reason why a lot of diplomatic wives don't bother to lean the language of the country they're in. Another is that things work against their learning it because they always move within the same kind of social environment. Diplomats recreate Little England or Little America around them wherever they move.

Abby -
Well, for the rest of us, culture shock greets you the moment you're off the plane.

Isabelle -
It's good to have a label to put on it, although I've never quite believed in culture shock.

Lena -
I didn't believe in it either, although I'd been warned about it even before I left home. And when I got here I went to one of those US embassy coffee mornings for wives, and we were given a two-page table, month by month, about what we should expect to feel.

'The first month you're supposed to be feeling exhilarated, the second month you start getting depressed, bewildered, disenchanted and restless. By the third month, you're downright discouraged and your aggro's coming out real strong; then it gradually gets better and it looks as if you might survive after all. By the time you've got back to normal, it's time to move on, or go back home.

Amanda -
The trouble is, if you read something like that, especially if it's been prepared by experts, you immediately develop all the symptoms they describe, irrespective of whether you are actually going through culture shock.

Abby -
Yes, that's the problem. On the other hand it may help some women who are feeling bewildered by their inability to cope to feel a bit

better knowing that it just may be due to something real - like knowing you have the 'flu rather than some strange, unnamed illness.

EG -
Culture shock is very real for a lot of people who go to live abroad, especially if it's the first time. But, from what a lot of women have told us, it may happen every time you go to a different country.

'A lot of research has been done about it on both sides of the Atlantic and nowadays it's taken a bit more seriously by employers because it has been a factor in breakdowns and depressions and has caused whole families to pack up and go home before their time is up - which is expensive for employers and gives transfers a bad name.

MJ -
Experts seem to agree, don't they, that there are several phases before one starts to adapt?

EG -
Yes, it's a process that develops over several months and goes through three main stages: a very active first period, during which you rush about getting things settled. During this period there is also a definite receptiveness - you're trying to give the place every chance, you're keeping an open mind.

'Then, as things are settling and the adrenalin wears off you enter the second stage, which is perhaps the most difficult. One of the experts, a Canadian psychologist called James Tyhurst, calls this the stage of "psychological arrival". People get increasingly anxious and depressed. They withdraw, they get hostile, they're no longer giving the place a chance. They start thinking of the people in their host country in terms of stereotypes. And they feel more and more helpless.

Abby -
I know women who've been here ten years and have never got past that stage!

EG -
Fortunately most people seem eventually to emerge from this second stage. Then the third phase is a phase of adaptation and adjustment to reality.

Isabelle -
Curiously, the stages you've just described are very close to the

stages people go through after a bereavement: there's a feeling of unreality and activity at first, then a stage of depression and finally an acceptance of reality.

EG -
Absolutely. And this has, in fact, been confirmed by psychologists. Mobility - especially international mobility - is an upheaval and can in many ways be compared to a bereavement. And though people vary in the way they cope and though circumstances also vary, knowing about culture shock may help a lot of newcomers to mobility feel less miserable about it or less guilty at not being able to cope.

Abby -
The American Women's Club organizes lectures and discussions about culture shock. They're very good. But I know, from having served on the Committee there, that there's a whole segment of American women who come and, literally within a few months, pack up and go home. I write or call them, but they've gone back already. Either there are reasons we know nothing about or they're feeling so distraught about not being able to cope with all the strangeness that they pack up and go. People don't talk about it much - it's too close to the bone - but I know for certain that there's a whole segment of American women who never fully "arrive".

Emma -
I'm afraid I don't have much sympathy with that. I think it's all a question of attitude. If you're sent to a foreign country, then you take it for granted from the start that things are going to be completely different. You don't go there expecting them to be the same as in Reading or St Louis, Missouri.

Abby -
Oh, I think you have to be a bit more understanding than that. You probably travelled a lot when you were a child. You probably come from that sort of background. A lot of people haven't had that chance. A woman coming from a smallish city in the Mid-West, say, who's always heard about how glamorous Europe is, and suddenly finds herself in a bourgeois suburb of Brussels or a poky little apartment in Paris, and she can't speak the language, and she doesn't know anybody.... She's gonna find it tough, I can tell you!

Isabelle -
I run a centre for women here and I have always refused to organize anything specifically for foreigners. But on the other hand I would very much like foreign women to come there, because joining is a good way of getting "into" a country. What I've always reacted

against is foreigners putting themselves in the position of foreigners.

MJ -
That's perhaps more of a long-term policy. You mustn't forget the first shocks when you arrive somewhere where practically everything's strange.

Isabelle -
I have to admit, when I think back a long time, that on our first move abroad - which was to England - I must have come as close to suffering from a kind of culture shock as I'll ever come. But that was because I found that I could not rely on my automatic everyday responses. I kept stepping off the pavement into the street looking the wrong way. And I didn't feel confident enough to drive for a long time. I felt I had to be on my guard all the time. It was quite upsetting, really.

Lena -
I never quite believed in culture shock either. After all, when you've lived in New York.... There can be few cities that are so cosmopolitan. However there were times when there was no other word to describe how I felt. It was a spacey feeling, a feeling of total isolation and helplessness. I felt there was no area in which I could function properly. If there was one thing I was good at at home, it was cooking. But you should have seen my first few meals in a Belgian kitchen. Flours behaved differently, sugars behaved differently, oven temperatures behaved differently, recipes worked differently. I would bring home what I thought was cream cheese - it would turn out to be something else. I felt totally inadequate.

MJ -
But in the long-term, I do agree with Isabelle. I personally feel very antagonistic to the way so many expatriates live in ghettoes and have the nerve to be hostile to the people whose country they're living in.

Abby -
I agree with you, but you've also got to remember that it's easier that way for a lot of people, especially if they're moving on. There's something very reassuring about living in a ghetto. It's familiar, you know what's going on, you can understand the social codes, you know what goes into the food you're eating, you play familiar sports and celebrate Thanksgiving and Independence Day almost exactly as you would in Richmond, Virginia. And, if you're lucky, as we are in Brussels, you'll even find American products, so there will be the minimum of adapting to do. I have no patience with it

myself, though, and I say to women who live like that "For God's sake, if you can't find a specific American flour, use the Belgian equivalent!"

MJ -
This sort of thing doesn't just happen with people who live in foreign enclaves. It happens to others as well, who have adjusted to living abroad in many ways. You'll find British women who've integrated reasonably well, yet who, if given the chance, will still buy Mother's Pride bread or Golden Syrup simply because it will remind them of home.

'We've had many British women saying how surprised they'd been by the fact that they wanted to go to "patriotic" events, like St David's Day celebrations or the Queen's Birthday party at the Embassy, or the Edinburgh Tattoo on the Grand' Place - things they would never have dreamt of doing at home. Even I find myself organizing carol-singing evenings around Christmas time, which I would never have done in England. It's a way of keeping in touch with one's own culture and of making sure that one's children do so too.

Amanda -
Yes, but it's also a form of homesickness, even if you're not quite aware of it. I often say to myself that I don't know what home-sickness is, because I don't actively miss being in the States, but I find myself longing at times for the oddest or silliest things, like tofu bean cakes or a typically American brand of supermarket soap. So I guess that's some form of homesickness.

MJ -
Homesickness may be too strong a term for it maybe, but it is odd the things people miss. Nobody but the British, for instance, would understand when I say I miss Marmite.

Abby -
What's that, for God's sake?

EG -
It's that disgusting brown stuff you put on toast.

Emma -
I understand what you mean: one often misses nursery-type food, things that really remind you of home.

Lena -
It's true. I miss my mother's lemon meringue pie. I wrote to her for

the recipe but when I made it, of course, it didn't taste at all like hers. But I also miss the kind of cheesecake you can only get in some New York delicatessen.

Abby -
Don't talk to me about New York delicatessen! Right now I'd sell myself for a plate of bagles and lox, or pastrami on rye!

Emma -
I remember when we were living in the Cameroons, with all that sunshine, the thing I missed most were those awful winter walks with the pram on Hampstead Heath. They were always in the rain - which at the time I didn't enjoy one little bit. But when I was in Africa, I felt that I just longed to be trudging along Hampstead Heath in wellington boots in the rain.

MJ -
I miss British humour. I suppose that's to do with a form of communication: the banter, the quick to-and-fro exchange that can only really take place in one's own language.

Abby -
But you can miss that even within your own language. I can tell you I missed New York humour when I was in California.

Lena -
You had a question in your questionnaire, didn't you, that dealt with what women missed. Did you find there was a pattern there?

EG -
There was a definite general pattern in that the overwhelming majority of the women said they missed their family and friends and things that directly relate to being in one's own country - a feeling of belonging, an ability to communicate. Food and cultural items came next. As you said earlier, Emma, nursery, or homey food: baked beans, sausages and Oxo cubes for the British, for instance. But also good manners on the road, public libraries, adult education classes, American theatre, British humour. One woman wrote that she missed British bus conductors and old ladies in bus queues. Some Americans missed very practical things, like waste-disposal systems. And then of course, land-scapes, or a sunny climate. The British in particular seemed to long for the English countryside. One woman, who lived in the Nether-lands, wrote that she just hadn't realized what an absence of sea and rocks could do to the soul.

MJ -
Before we all dissolve into homesickness, where were we?

Abby -
I'd like to say something that occurred to me when we were talking about certain foreign communities that live in their little golden ghettoes. I think that for a lot of them, apart from making them feel less insecure, it's a policy decision: they don't want to move out of the ghetto because they want to be able to slide right back into their lives when they go home. You know among us Americans, counter-culture shock has about as bad a name as culture shock.

'When you're back in the States, even just on a visit, you find that you live in very different worlds and that you have nothing in common to talk about if you've been living in a foreign country and mixing with other nationalities. And if you tell them about what you've been doing, like how you went skiing in Switzerland at Christmas, they will think you're showing off. They'll say: "You've come back with a very snotty attitude."

'I have to tell you that I'm quite nervous about going back to live in the States. My husband's company's thinking of sending us to California. My husband will still be travelling a lot and he's concerned about me, because there's nothing in the desert of California. The nearest airport is two hours away. I can learn to dance like a hillbilly, carry a gun, but I think I shall just wither up and die! You don't know what this place is like. There's just nothing. It looks like a one-horse town in a Western - John Wayne coming out of the saloon.

'We went to visit the place a couple of weeks ago. They all drive these pick-up vans there, with guns hanging in the window, and Hans said: "You'll have to learn to shoot." "Shoot what?", I said, "Rabbits?" "No," he said, "not rabbits. People." "People?" "Yes, people."

'Hans says they'll give us a beautiful house with an olympic swimming-pool, four acres of land, a couple of horses, a couple of dogs. And three guns. "Why?" I said. "For protection", he said. "Against what?" "Against the people who will break in and rob."

MJ -
The thought of going home is frightening for a lot of people, even if they haven't got such dramatic reasons as yours for not wanting to go.

EG -
The trouble is that when you've been living abroad for a while, there

may not be anywhere you can really call home. A lot of women have told us that they felt a bit like strangers in their own countries, and that people at home felt they had changed and that they no longer fitted in. On the other hand they also remain foreigners in the country they live in. Of course some people integrate better than others; and some don't mind not belonging as much as others.

Lena -
It's sometimes a very unreal feeling. I often felt, before my son was born, that I was living in parentheses. That this was a period which did not belong to the real fabric of my life.

Amanda -
I think that for a lot of people the feeling of unreality also comes from the fact that, on the whole, expatriates have a much higher standard of living than they do at home. This may not be true of some Americans, who have a very high standard of living in the States, but it certainly seems to be true of Europeans and diplomatic people from the Third World.

MJ -
Yes, a lot of women mentioned this feeling of unreality in their questionnaires. One of them even referred to the money her husband was earning as "Monopoly money".

Isabelle -
This is the reason why I think it is so important for foreigners to make the effort to get involved in the country they are living in. From little things, such as buying local newspapers to big things such as taking sides. I always try to take sides. In America I took sides for Kennedy against Nixon. I couldn't belong to any party, but I took sides all the same. And I felt happier about this than if I had just sat back and watched.

MJ -
Unfortunately the people whose country you're living in may not want you to take sides. I remember going to a pro-abortion march here with an American friend who was carrying a banner, and some woman in the crowd angrily tore the banner from her hand, shouting: "What do you think you're doing meddling in our affairs, you foreigner?"

Emma -
People in the diplomatic service can never get truly involved anyway. But I do agree that the standard of living of expatriates has a part to play, both in their own feeling of unreality and in the way they are perceived by the people in their host country. It becomes

another barrier between you, and that's especially true of some European countries where we're much better off than a lot of them. Southern or Eastern European countries, for instance. When we were in Hungary and we were quite young, we made a lot of friends of our own age who were Hungarian writers and artists, with whom we felt we really could communicate on quite a deep level. But I always found it nervewracking to invite them to our flat. It was very luxurious by their standards and we had a maid who waited at meal times. I found that dreadful and embarrassing and I think it made them ill at ease. It was that, more than other cultural aspects, like language difficulties, that made me feel I was truly an alien.

MJ -
I feel this alienness at the political level. Had I stayed in the U.K., I would have been involved politically at grass-roots level. But here we can't even vote. One woman we talked to said she felt she was living in never-never land. And I can identify with that.

EG -
Yes, but don't forget that women were very divided on that point. Whilst many told us that they hated their lack of involvement, both in what was going on in their own countries and in their host countries, there were many others who said that they felt freer. Freer from the social or political constrictions of their own culture, freer from their mothers, freer from their in-laws. As foreigners, they felt they could get away with a lot of things and from a lot of things. Of course, the other side of the coin is that one ends up feeling that one doesn't belong anywhere.

Emma -
All I can say is that those women couldn't have been diplomatic wives. I feel much less free than if I were at home, partly because diplomatic wives are still to some extent expected to play a certain role, although fewer and fewer are prepared to play it. I do it sometimes, although at no great cost to myself, I must say, because it's not my real self. At a cocktail party or a dinner I quite consciously put myself "away" for the evening and I play at being someone else and hope that someone will strike a spark.

'The amount and type of diplomatic duties differ from place to place of course. In some places, like Brussels, there are no demands whatsoever. In other places, like Africa, or Hungary, or Moscow, there were enormous demands on me as an embassy wife.

'And oh the joy of being back in England when we were on home leave; of being able to eat spaghetti with friends round the kitchen table instead of having these long, formal dinners; of not having to worry about what you're saying, about whether your conversations are being tape-recorded or your telephone calls monitored. This sort of thing becomes a strain when you're living with it all the time. In the diplomatic service you do have to be careful about what you're saying. There is a certain sense of having to behave yourself, having to worry about your husband's reputation, put on the right smile and not lose your temper with people. There is a certain sense that you ought to be on your best behaviour, and that is a bore. It's more than that - it's a responsibility; it's a husband's career that's at stake if his wife gets drunk or starts behaving in an outrageous way.

MJ -
Do you find that the constraints of diplomatic life affect your friendships?

Emma -
Most of my closest friends have nothing to do with the diplomatic service, so these constraints are minimal. But - and I am sure this won't come as any news to you - what I do find affects friendships is not so much the constraints of diplomatic life as the very transience of the life you lead when you're forever shunted here and there. I try not to let this affect my involvement with people, but without realizing you find yourself standing back a little from relationships that, given time and opportunity, could develop into strong friendships. In our kind of life you learn to expect relationships to be cut off by moving, and if you're self-protective, you won't get too involved. Nevertheless, I'm happy to say that some relationships do develop into friendships that defy distance and transience.

MJ -
A lot of women have told us they thought that transience prevented them from making close friendships. We had a question about it in the questionnaire. I remember one woman even wrote that she felt like a submarine that cruised along but did not surface.

EG -
Just over fifty percent of the respondents said that about transience - which is significant, I think, and partly responsible for the overwhelming feeling of isolation these women said they felt.

Abby -
I don't feel like that at all. In fact I feel quite the opposite. I've met people I would never have met, all sorts of nationalities. And I've made pretty deep friendships. Even if some of my friends have gone back home or have moved on, we keep in touch.

MJ -

It's obvious that living abroad puts a lot of strain on relationships and causes a certain number of constraints. What, do you think, are the advantages of living abroad, as opposed to those of staying in one's own country?

Abby -

For me, the main advantage is that it satisfies both my curiosity about the world and the fact that I like challenges. Living abroad - especially if you're called upon to move every now and then - is a constant challenge. You can never afford to become complacent about anything, least of all yourself.

Emma -

I would tend to agree with you there, but the problem is that if you move too often, your feeling of curiosity and challenge may become blunted by weariness. I too think I have a much more interesting group of friends than I would have had had I remained in England because they are from different places. I enjoy the mixture of nationalities you get in the diplomatic milieu, but I also very much enjoy the multi-cultural aspect of some cities such as Brussels or Paris. It's a challenge, it appeals to my imagination, it opens me up in many ways. It prevents me from taking things for granted as I invariably do when I'm back in Britain.

'Usually, when we've been on a posting for quite a while, it becomes obvious that, of the two of us - my husband and myself - I am the one who's having the more interesting time. But of course this takes a long time to build up, and it's this perpetual destruction that's getting to me now.

Lena -

For me, one of the advantages of living abroad is that you are able to take a long cool look at your own country. Because you're put in the position of being a foreigner you become aware of how others see you. Now you may disagree with them, but in the process of reviewing their reasons you may come upon aspects of your country that you never questioned. And I think that's beneficial.

MJ -

Yes, other people also have said that this was one of the more interesting side effects of living abroad. But why did you all go abroad in the first place. Was it a joint decision on your part and your husband's? What were your motivations?

Isabelle -

We went abroad for adventure's sake. I liked the idea of travelling

and so did my husband. We didn't have any children at the time so
we were quite free. Of course we had to weigh up whether we
wanted to stay in the kind of life we knew, where we would be near
our families and where, indeed, I would be able to carry on with the
career and future I was hoping for - or whether we wanted to go out
into the blue. And it seemed very much more of a challenge to go
out into the blue. The much larger salary my husband was offered
was certainly important, but it was definitely not the main reason.
I think the main reason was that the challenge was something more
open-ended.

Lena -
As my husband was being sent abroad on a three-year contract, I
decided to look on it as a chance for a long holiday. I felt I had
plateaued out in my work and needed to do something about it, but
I didn't know what. This was a sort of breathing space, a time for
taking stock of myself.

Abby -
Oh, I just leapt at it! Europe, Vienna, travel.... I was fired at the
whole idea.

Emma -
I never questioned it because we married straight after Cambridge
and Colin went into the Foreign Office, so I knew we would be
posted abroad. I was wholly for it.

Amanda -
This may not be what you wanted to hear, but going overseas was
a release for me. I was finding that I couldn't go on acting and
looking after my kids at the same time, so being posted abroad
eliminated that conflict.

MJ -
This seems to be true of quite a few women whose lives prior to the
move were in some sort of conflict. Going abroad then can get
people out of certain dilemmas.

Isabelle -
Yes, I have met women who felt that. The danger here, however, is
that going abroad may be a kind of escape. In French we call it *une
fuite en avant*. An escape not from circumstances, but from oneself.
And that is always dangerous.

Abby -
What about you two ladies? You're also camp-followers. What
made you go abroad?

MJ -

When my husband got a job in Brussels I thought we were only going away for two years, and I thought, "Well, for two years, I'll give it a try." But in fact I was kidding myself because I knew jolly well that it was an open-ended contract. But the only way I could face it was to pretend to myself it was only for two years.

Emma -

So you went reluctantly.

MJ -

Yes, I did really. But part of me nevertheless was excited about living on the continent. What about you, Enid?

EG -

I was not only reluctant, I was absolutely furious. I didn't want to live anywhere in the world but Paris - I was extremely happy there. But my husband was fired with the idea of working for Europe and I didn't feel that I could stand in his way, especially since my work - which was freelance translating and writing - was perfectly portable. I simply had no excuse.

MJ -

If you're not on an equal economic basis with your husband, how can you say no? Perhaps on the third or fourth move you might stand up for yourself, but it's very difficult on the first.

EG -

How possible do you think it is for your husbands to say no to a transfer or posting?

Emma -

We did that once. We asked to stay in London when we came back from Africa. I said everyone could do what they wanted, but I was going to stay in England to get myself a qualification so that I wouldn't be an unemployed wife in the future.

'I had decided, when we were in Africa, that there was no way I was going to go abroad again without something of my own to do. So on that particular home leave that we'd asked for, I took a photography training course and now my photography and my writing are my lifebelt. At the end of a morning in the dark room, at least you have some pictures to see. It's creative, but it's also more than that: it's a personal record, a record of time spent, which might otherwise be wasted - a reason for being there.

'I also found it very useful in diplomatic life to have an alibi. You've got to be doing something in order to be able to refuse things you don't want to do, like going to tea parties or coffee mornings and so on. But, to go back to your question, Colin could certainly not indefinitely refuse postings without jeopardizing his career.

MJ -
Abby, what about you?

Abby -
Well, I'd dearly love to refuse to go to California if and when they finally decide to send us there. But although my husband's employers say they don't penalize you for refusing a transfer, I know for a fact that they do. They won't openly say anything, but you'll be blocked somewhere and they'll hold it against you.

MJ -
Isabelle?

Isabelle -
I am sure that it would be possible for my husband to refuse a transfer - at least once anyway - but it's a question of whether he would actually want to do so. His career is important to him, he loves what he's doing. As you know, we've found a solution which, although far from ideal, still respects our individual wishes.

Abby -
Ah, but you see, my husband's employers would not put up with that sort of solution. They're a very patriarchal firm. They don't want to be seen as a breaker-up of family life. And besides they think the wife must be a good support for the husband.

EG -
Nevertheless more and more women are refusing to follow their husbands abroad, and this is a pressure on employers that's making them review their attitudes, accept other ways of living and evolve different policies. Things have changed so much in the last twenty years: more and more women expect to have jobs and careers, not be dependents.

MJ -
So what is the solution? Do you think there can be an answer that's valid for everyone?

Emma -
How can there ever be that? That's simply not possible. Everyone's circumstances are different, everyone reacts differently. What I feel to be acceptable may be anathema to the next person. People have

to make up their own minds about their lives and their options.

MJ -
Well, let me try to put it another way. Would you do it again? Would you be willing, tomorrow, to follow your husband to another country?

Abby -
Yes, definitely - but not to the backwoods of California!

Lena -
No, I don't think so. I want my son to grow up in his own country, and I want to take up my career again. I feel this experience has been beneficial in the long run, but I now feel ready to take up the reins of my life again and this I can only do in my own country.

Amanda -
Yes, without hesitation. Moving around has become my life. We feel we have a foot in the States anyway because we've just built ourselves a house in California, but I don't think right now that living in just one place for years and years would satisfy me. What about the two of you? Has working on this project changed your mind in any way about following your husbands somewhere else?

MJ -
Well, it has certainly enabled me, for one, to sort out my own feelings on the subject. And the answer to the question of whether I'd do it again is, no, I'm afraid I wouldn't - unless I could have the certainty of having a good job. Enid, what about you?

EG -
If it happened right away I think I'd stand up for myself and say no, unless it was absolutely vital for my husband. The reason for this is that I went back to university a few years ago and I am training in Brussels in something that's extremely important to me. If the opportunity to move elsewhere came up once I've finished my training, then I might very well say yes, provided, of course, that I could practice wherever we were sent.

Emma -
How well I understand that! Having a profession that I can carry on my back anywhere has made all the difference to me. It's a lifebelt, but it's not just that. It's what I'd probably choose to do anyway wherever I was. But to answer your question, I am not sure how I feel about another move after this new one to Paris. It's a question of how many times we've moved. We've moved too many times. After five years in Paris I may be happy and ready to move

again. But right now I am resenting moving, and with children it
becomes more complicated. You become obsessed with the children's education. As opposed to a lot of foreign service people we
never did send our children to public school in England. I was
always adamant about not breaking up the family. But it does pose
certain problems.

Isabelle -
I told you what my attitude to further moves was already. But to go
back to a question that Morwenna had asked earlier - whether
there is some sort of general answer that could apply to everyone
- I wonder whether what is true for all of us here is that the answer
depends on the stage you're at in your life, and perhaps the stage
in your relationship with your husband. At the beginning I wanted
to move, I was happy to follow my husband. And then came a time
when I wanted to achieve something of my own, for myself. And this
in the end became more important than keeping the family
together.

'Thirty years ago I didn't have this kind of nagging obsession with
work. It catches up on you later on. This is something you don't
think about when you first decide to go and live abroad, and
everything is a challenge, and the salary's much bigger, so you
think you can lead a much easier life than at home.... But then, you
can't live your life in retrospect.'

2

A Binding Force

Margaret was silent. London was but a foretaste of that nomadic civilisation which is altering human nature so profoundly, and throws upon human relations a strain greater than they have ever borne before. Under cosmopolitanism, if it comes, we shall receive no help from the earth. Trees and meadows and mountains will only be a spectacle, and the binding force that they once exercised on character must be entrusted to Love alone. May Love be equal to the task !

E.M. Forster,
Howard's End, London, 1910

The women who took part in the group discussion that follows were Monica, 37, American; Judy, 46, British; Esther, 36, British; Antonia, 31, American; Elvira, 42, Venezuelan; and Polly, 46, British, who, after a number of years in Geneva, returned to Britain, where she heard about our project; during a visit to Belgium she contacted us in order to participate in a group discussion.

EG -
Polly's presence here tonight and the story she will tell us later on, make us feel that it would be a good opportunity to concentrate tonight's discussion on what mobility does to the personal relationships within a family - between husband and wife and parents and children.

'It is evident from almost all the cases we've seen so far in our research that, when one moves abroad, the family - that is the immediate family group - has to rely far more on itself than it would do at home. It is cut off from the larger family group, from friends, other connections and its own culture, and it has to survive in what is usually at first a completely alien environment. This makes family members far more dependent on one another, which may change the balance of roles in some ways, or add a further weight to existing roles. I don't want to dwell on a subject that's probably familiar to all of you, but, to put matters in a nutshell, I'd like to say by way of introduction to tonight's discussion that it's clear that mobility as expatriates experience it acts as a catalyst in a number of areas, family relationships being one of the major areas affected.

'We'd like to hear your views about it, but as the subject is vast and convoluted it might be best to start off with how moves affect relationships between husbands and wives and get on to the subject of children later. Esther, would you like to start?

Esther -
Yes. Well I'm Esther, I'm 36 years old, British, married to a businessman, and we have four children.

'I'd like to make it clear from the beginning that I followed Steve with a lot of agony, but I felt it was absolutely my duty. Curiously, one of the reasons why we left Britain (although this was not actually openly voiced at the time) was that Steve was - is - very close to his family and it was becoming claustrophobic. After all these years I'm still in two minds about the extended family: on the one hand you want the support system it offers, but on the other it's claustrophobic. From the children's point of view, of course, it's very sad... But anyway it was Steve's choice to move, not mine. He's a great francophile and had always wanted to go and work in

France. As it happened, however, the job he was offered was in Belgium, but Brussels was one step nearer to Paris than London, so he took it immediately.

'I know exactly what you meant when you said, just now, that when a family moves abroad it becomes cut off. In our case we cut ourselves off almost literally by selling our house in England. We had to sell it because the firm that took Steve on was Belgian - which meant that we had his salary but no allowances.The firm didn't even pay for our furniture to be moved out. Had we not sold the house, I don't quite know what we would have done.

'I resented it very much. I felt I couldn't forgive Steve - which was quite unfair of me. I think the house meant roots to me, but also, quite concretely, selling it stopped our flexibility. It meant that we couldn't go back, that we were marooned here.

'So you could say that from the very beginning, even before we actually got to Brussels, the move put a strain on our relationship.

'When we arrived in Belgium, things went from bad to worse. Steve had decided to buy a house in Brussels because that's what we'd done at home, but immediately afterwards the bottom dropped out of the housing market, so we were stuck even deeper, with a house we couldn't even hope to sell.

'We bought it in October 1978 at an auction sale. It was a fairly derelict house and, as we drove away from the auction, we said: "We won't have any more children". (We already had two, you see.) And then, a few days later, I discovered I was pregnant. Then both our cars crashed and, to top it all, soon after the baby was born, Steve's company folded up. He struggled on to try and make some sort of niche here for himself, and eventually got a job - not in Brussels, but in Paris. There was no question of the rest of us moving along with him, so for two years he commuted between Paris and Brussels, coming back at week-ends to be with us.

MJ -
How did that affect your relationship?

Esther -
Oh, drastically, I think. In the beginning moving abroad increased very much my dependence on him, and Steve is actually someone who doesn't like people to be dependent on him, so that, of course, created all sorts of problems. But when he went off to Paris, I found myself having to cope with everything entirely on my own, and I started getting more independent. Now if Steve doesn't go away for

at least two days every week, I feel absolutely claustrophobic. And other women whose husbands commute from one city to another have said the same thing to me. Once you get into this sort of lifestyle you may find that it suits you very well. At the most basic level it means that you can sit in bed and pluck your eyebrows without causing any derogatory comment, or sit for three hours in the bath with a novel, go and see your friends, go to W.O.E.* - anything. You've got your autonomy and no one's there to contest it or interfere.

'But it was different for him, of course, because he didn't have a base here. He didn't have time to build his own contacts and develop his own activities and he didn't have close personal friends as I did. He became resentful of the activities I had developed, and even more so when I refused to drop them when he eventually came back to live in Brussels.

'So you see, you build up your own independence not so much because you want to, but because you have to. You become self-reliant. It is difficult to analyze exactly how all this changed me. I think it was the forced beginnings of a growing-up process, and also being forced to face myself. It made me more adventurous, it made me find friends and learn to rely on friends rather than family. What I cannot work out, however, is how different this is from what any woman of the same age in England is going through.

MJ -
This is a recurrent question, isn't it, that women living abroad ask themselves? Many of the changes we go through, like that growing-up process you were talking about, would most probably have occurred at some point or another at home. But certain things are speeded up or exaggerated when you live abroad and so perhaps one is forced into facing oneself sooner or more drastically than one might be at home.

Esther -
Yes. In fact both of us were forced into it as a result of the move. I mean Steve's changed a hell of a lot too. He was very successful in the U.K. and he absolutely dominated everything we did. All the problems he encountered after he came here, with his firm folding up and his having to find work, then starting his own business, being away from the children and me, my own independence - all that's made him more insecure. And life in Brussels is quite difficult for men who are self-employed and only moderately suc-cessful. All these fast-moving, high-flying middle-to-top manage-ment people you constantly meet.... They are usually much more "defined", if you understand what I mean, because they belong to

*Women's Organisation for Equality

huge, successful companies and they're moving up, up, up all the time.

'We were very different from most people here. Going abroad had no financial benefits for us, and a lot of people here - the expatriates, I mean - are much better off than us. We tended to stay away from them, but even so.... I'll never forget to the end of my days, asking a whole load of people to dinner, just as I might have done in London. It was a supper party for 21 people, and in the morning in the supermarket I bumped into a woman who was coming to dinner that evening, and she said: "I think you're so brave. I've only got matching things for eight". My mouth dropped open: It had never occurred to me that this could be a problem. She was from a completely different background, in which there was a lot of one-upmanship. We met a lot of people like that at first; in fact they tended to be the only people we met, and that increased my loneliness. Afterwards we learnt to avoid them.

Monica -
Forgive my probing, but did the strain on your relationship with your husband ever resolve itself?

Esther -
Yes, I suppose it did eventually but it took a long time and we both had to work at it quite hard. However, I think that we were both determined to make it succeed.

MJ -
Antonia, you were used to moving around as a child, weren't you? Did this in any way help your family relationships when you later started to move as a wife and mother?

Antonia -
I'll have to think about this for a minute.... Shall I start by saying who I am? Well my name's Antonia, I'm 31, American, and my husband's a Danish foreign correspondent. We have two children, a girl and a boy. Yes, we did move around all the time when I was a kid. My mother herself was an expatriate child, so you see, my own kids are third-generation expatriates. My father died when I was very little and then my mother joined the American Foreign Service and I went along with her wherever she was sent.

'My problem as a child was that I felt I didn't belong anywhere, and this was of course compounded by the fact that my mother doesn't belong anywhere either. I think perhaps if my father had lived I might have had more roots. But curiously, now that I am moving around with my husband and my own children, I seem to have found my roots. Or perhaps "made them", with the help of Peter and the kids. I mean, as you said earlier, when you live in a foreign country, and especially when you are moved around often as we are, the family's thrown together. You have to hang together, at least for a while. So our family's become our roots and our home, and I find that moving has made us all much closer.

'I feel very close to my husband, and very involved in everything he's doing. And he takes an enormous interest in the kids and spends as much time as he can with us. I think I did feel a certain amount of fear and resentment at the beginning when we were being moved from pillar to post by the newspaper. It was my childhood all over again. But because it's turned out so well, I have forgotten about it. Also I know that any negative feeling on my part would poison the children and my relationship with my husband.

MJ -
Judy? What's your experience?

Judy -
It's quite obvious from my own experience as well that when one moves abroad the family is completely thrown in on itself. I suppose it's a matter of survival at first, but I personally think it is potentially an extremely dangerous situation, because you may well end up living in a bubble.

'I forgot to introduce myself.... My name's Judy, I am 46, British, a teacher, and I have two boys who are now at university in Britain. My husband, Alan, is a businessman, working for a multinational.

'After university I started teaching, with every intention of making this my career. Then I met Alan, and, within a year we were married. I didn't give up my job after I had a baby, but when Alan started to work for an international cloth manufacturer and was suddenly transferred to France, I had no alternative but to take an enforced sabbatical. We thought it was only going to be for a year anyway.

'Alan was working in Lyons, and we thought we'd take advantage of the lovely countryside around it, so we rented a cottage outside a tiny village. It seemed idyllic at first - just the cows and the trees for company, and a one-year-old child. I had my second son there.

'Then the one year became two, and it went on like that. During those years I was increasingly involved with what Alan was doing. In my head I was fighting his battles. His life and his world were of total importance to me. They, and the kids were the centre of my life - indeed the only thing in my life.

'After four years life became so lonely out in the countryside that we actually moved into Lyons proper, and things began to change. I became involved with people there and the children went to the *école maternelle*. I began to run a playgroup along British lines. There was nothing like it in Lyons at the time and it went down well. So I started to forge my own life once more and to live less vicariously. Over all those years Alan was away a great deal, travelling all over the world, and he became increasingly involved in his work. When we were living in the cottage I used to dread his travelling; now, in Lyons, where I was making my own independent life, with friends and interests of my own, I began to welcome it.

'But of course, just as I was settling into a fulfilling, autonomous life, Alan's firm decided to transfer us. And that's when we really started to move. First within France, then to Italy, to Germany and finally to Belgium - altogether 13 times in 10 years.

'For a long time it never occurred to me to say no, because it was for Alan's job. He was the breadwinner, so we had to follow. At the time I was not particularly negative. I saw each move to a different country as a chance to see a different culture, and I managed to start teaching again properly - in some places it was teaching English as a foreign language; in other places, where they had British or American schools, it was history or English literature.

'But during all those years, unbeknown to us, the moves had been whittling away at our relationship. We went further and further from each other, and as the children grew, this became more marked.

'In fact my marriage right now is in a very precarious state, and it is hard for me to continue to speak as if I am going to remain married to Alan. But if we were to stay together and, tomorrow, he were to stand up and say: "I've been offered the post of a lifetime in...wherever..." I think that at this point, having been through all the things I've been through, I'd say "No, I'm not going. I under-stand what this might do to your career, but there are other things in my life now that are important to me, and I'm no longer prepared to make this kind of sacrifice for somebody else.'

Antonia -
What if his circumstances were such as to make a move imperative, would you still say no?

Judy -
I don't know.... If he were terribly unhappy in his present job, or if the situation were really catastrophic - i.e. if he was made

redundant or was unemployed, for instance - then I might be forced to make another decision. But if it's a question of going up one more step in the career ladder, I would say no, without any hesitation. I think I would feel strong enough to say "No, this is enough; we have all this, why do we need to have more?"

'The thing that strikes me as unacceptable now is that, as women, we are used all the time to putting somebody else's needs - usually a man's needs - before our own, and it's always a question of somehow making the best of a situation, swallowing a bitter pill and saying to ourselves "Well perhaps I'll get something out of it."

'None of us expatriates are exactly on the breadline. And if it's just a question of a bit more money here, or a bit more status there, why are we doing this? Why are we doing this to ourselves? Putting ourselves in a position where we are constantly making sacrifices, perpetuating this cycle of saying "It's for somebody else, and what that somebody else wants is more important than what I think is right for *me*." Career and money - these are the rationalizations. What's at stake here, really, is not the career or the money: it's the way we've been socialized - that socialization that says women must put men and children before their own needs. I think you have a right to your life, to have and make your own choices. Even if this means having to make do with less money, or less status. Maybe there are other things in your value system that are more important, like human relationships, where your children go to school, your house, your own work, stability....

EG -
This is perhaps the most crucial question that women in our situation have to face.

Monica -
Yes, but how many of them actually face it in the long run? As Judy said, women hide behind the rationalization that they're putting up with what is sometimes an unbearable situation for *his* career, *his* salary, *his* status.

EG -
Yes, but this may also be true of a lot of women who remain in their home countries and have to put up with different situations which may be hard on them because they've been brought up in the tradition that men and children come first in women's list of priorities. What I mean to say is, how much of the blame for the eventual collapse of a marital relationship can one lay at the door of mobility?

Judy -
This is a difficult problem to disentangle. I've given it a lot of thought. Some of it, to be sure, must be blamed on the way women have been socialized. But - and this is true in the case of my own marital relationship - a lot of the blame must be laid on mobility. Mobility changes people. It changes men. They are basically just as starved of meaningful relationships as us, though this is harder to detect because they have their professional structure and are in a fast upward lane. What they don't put into their social life - the emotions, that is, that one can put into close relationships with friends and family - they put in their ambition and energy at work. They become harder and more materialistic, they tend to get further and further away from their real selves. I think that they re-direct, or rather mis-direct, all that energy that at home might be channelled elsewhere. And as for the women - I can only talk of myself, but I know, from countless discussions I had with other women that I am not alone in feeling this way - if one didn't have to constantly uproot oneself and start making relationships all over again, if one did not have to live vicariously, if one could have the stability, the continuity, both at home and at work that most people have one might feel less angry, less resentful. This anger, just as the men's ambitions and materialism is, I think, a direct result of mobility.

MJ -
Monica, why don't you tell us who you are and what you feel about all this?

Monica -
Well, my name, as you know, is Monica, I am 37, American - from Ohio, actually - I trained as a science teacher; my husband works for a large corporation and we have three kids, aged 14 down to 6. We've been living abroad since the early days of our marriage and we ended up in Brussels four years ago.

'I feel pretty much like Judy about moving - what it does to people, both men and women, although my experience is different from hers in many ways.

'I come from a large family, back in the States: four brothers, one sister, very loving parents and a busy social life. Although I was away during my college years, home was always a very important base to me. I hadn't realized, until I came to Europe, just how used I was to having constant human contact - and supportive contact at that.

'So I got married to Jerry and, soon after that his firm moved us to

England. I went from a very stable and busy family and social life to a country where I didn't know a soul and where, I soon found out, I couldn't even get a job. We didn't have children at the time, so we were thrown in on ourselves as a couple as well. And although this made us closer at first, our experiences after a while became so different that, almost from the start, you could say that the move had begun to affect our relationship.

'At least there wasn't a language problem, but there was a great deal of culture shock nevertheless, and all the greater because I expected that speaking English would have shielded me from a lot of that. There were times when I thought, "To hell with this. I'm going to get the first plane home. None of this is shaping up as I'd expected."

'I don't think Jerry had any real idea about how torn and disappointed and lost I felt. Of course I'd talk about it, but he simply could not relate to what I was going through. He'd gone into a challenging job, with a big corporation, which fully occupied him and it was strange to him that I had these feelings at all. And, of course, the fact that he was so absorbed put me out further.

'There were a few incidents that rankled particularly. There was one occasion, for instance, where he'd gone over to Washington for four days' work. I went to meet his plane at Heathrow, and he wasn't there. What had happened was that he'd missed the plane, tried to contact me, but I was already on my way down to London, and then he got so involved talking to people that he didn't bother to let me know later that he intended to catch the first flight out the next morning. I was beside myself with worry, thinking he'd had an accident. I phoned his firm in Washington, and nobody knew where he was - they must have thought I was crazy. Then the next day he walked in without any misgivings.

'These things - a combination of total absorption with his work, and a lack of accountability - make it very difficult for one to distinguish where personality problems end and problems linked with mobility start.

'What I do know is that whatever the problems, they are made worse by the fact that one's living in a foreign country. I definitely think that being separated from my family - this close, warm unit - and not having any other form of support group, made small problems like this incident seem much larger than they were. They generated a resentment that only grew and grew as the years went by.

'In order to regain some control over my life I decided to do something about making my qualifications more acceptable to the British, so I set about taking every course I could. But this didn't lead anywhere concrete.

'I got to the point where I no longer gave a damn about what happened to my husband's career. In any case by then all the excitement had gone out of it for him. He'd met a few blocks after those early euphoric days. But he was still keen on all those materials benefits he got out of it, both as a corporation executive and as an expatriate - his big salary, his beautiful home, his garden, his two cars. Meanwhile I was becoming increasingly nasty, and finally I think Jerry realized he had to do something about it. I don't know how he managed it, but he got transferred - not back to the States as I'd always hoped, but to the next best place: Brussels.

'We had heard from other company members who'd spent time there that Brussels was a kind of heaven for expatriates. The international community there was truly international and very well organized and there were lots of job openings for expatriate wives, even American ones who did not have the same advantages to start with as Europeans. Had we not made the change when we did, I don't know what would have happened. I feel my mental balance was in question.

'Anyway, we came here, and I was very, very happy. Adjusting to Belgium was easy. The way of life was just what I had been missing all those years in England. I was mixing with all sorts of nationalities. Even the foreign languages were a challenge. But the most important thing was that I found loads of people on the same wavelength as me. They'd moved from their country, they were positive. This was immediate stimulation to me.

'I started studying French immediately, then got to grips with the job market, which I found was not as "open" to Americans as I had been led to believe. By then I realized I had to grab any opportunities that came along, and I did land quite an interesting P.R. job.

'As luck would have it, the happier and more fulfilled I became, the sulkier Jerry became. He didn't - doesn't - like Belgium. The Birmingham way of life suited his temperament better - or rather being an American in Birmingham did. Here, whenever he has a problem, with bureaucracy, or superiors, or whatever, it gets thrown in my face, because I kind of forced his hand to move away from England. So instead of bringing us together - which I'd hoped the move to Brussels would - it has set us even further apart.

'I suppose each move has tended to reveal some of the truth about us - about each of us, and about both of us as a couple - mainly that we were not that compatible to start with. It has certainly shown me that I was too passive. I'd put up with a lot of mental anguish for the sake of his career. Oh, I was noisy about it, I made a lot of fuss, I must have been insufferable at times - but basically I was passive. And he was indifferent, or unwilling to really listen to what I was trying to tell him. If one is in a dependent position, as I was, then the person who is in the dominant position, in the controlling position, doesn't have to take any notice of you.

Esther -
Are there any married relationships that truly profit from moving?

MJ -
We have certainly talked to women who said that their marital relationship had become closer as a result of going to live abroad. Many of these women, however, had experienced what, for want of a better word, we call the "one-off" move - i.e. they moved abroad once, and for a determined period of time - or were living abroad indefinitely. But we also did meet a few "perpetual nomads" - not many, I must admit - who thought that as long as they could develop their own life and interests, or channel their creative energy into work or an occupation of some kind, their marriage had a good chance of surviving their many moves intact.

EG -
But here again, this is something that can be said of any marriage anywhere. If both partners are fulfilled and autonomous, there's a good chance that a marriage will thrive.

'The point about mobility, it seems to me, is that it is a catalyst. It often draws couples closer together at first because they are a little lost in a strange environment. But it is later that it really reveals itself as a catalyst. If a marriage is basically working and both partners start getting something positive out of their new environ-ment, the move has a good chance of strengthening the relation-ship. But if there are cracks, it might well show them up - and more clearly so than at home, where cracks can be filled with the help of mutual support structures.

'Over and above that, however, mobility adds a lot of strains that can affect a relationship - circumstantial strains that might never have happened at home - such as a wife suddenly finding herself not only in an unfamiliar place, but in an unfamiliar situation, such as being at home all day, minding the children and the household where perhaps at home she was a career woman, with quite a different timetable and personal status.

Polly -
I agree with you about moving being a catalyst, but I think it goes beyond showing up cracks in couples. It shows up the cracks in any of us, men or women, and adds other cracks of its own. In the case of my own family, moving abroad was catastrophic, with long-lasting effects that we're still feeling. However this is a long story, and as it has more to do with children than with husband-wife relationship, I'd rather talk about it later.

MJ -
Elvira, you are, because of your husband's profession, called upon to move from country to country quite frequently. Has this in any way affected your relationship with your husband?

Elvira -
I think I belong to that category of women who feel that moves can be beneficial to everyone concerned. But I suppose I'd better start by saying who I am.

'My name is Elvira, I am 42, and I come from Caracas, Venezuela. My husband is a diplomat and we have had postings in all five continents in the twenty years we have been married. Our eldest son is twenty, and at university in the United States and our two youngest, who are fifteen and twelve are here with us. We have been in Brussels for three years.

'As my husband was already in the diplomatic service when I married him - there is a ten-year difference in age between us - the idea of moving around the world was very definitely part of the understanding of what our marriage was going to be like. So, although until then I had had no direct experience of living in a foreign country, I was quite geared to it.

'Despite his profession, my husband is quite a shy man, and my role in this marriage is the same as it would have been had we remained in our own country: it is in a way to be a communicator for him, a forger of human contacts. This is something that comes quite naturally to me and which I enjoy. His role, on the other hand, is to be the one who shields the family from material and concrete problems, a paternal - but, I strongly feel, not paternalistic - role. Thus, it is the fact that each of us has this definite role which corresponds perfectly to the persons we are deep down, and somehow protects the other, that has made our marriage strong.

'My husband has always encouraged me to do what I feel like doing, in terms of occupation, friendships, commitments, so I have not felt real frustration in any of our moves, except, of course, for the sadness of leaving friends that I make - but that I have always accepted as being one of the drawbacks of the kind of life we lead. And there are always ways of keeping in touch.

'I feel there are a lot of positive aspects to our life. Principally, as far as I am concerned, there is the possibility of self-renewal. I agree with all of you when you say that no move leaves somebody unchanged. You are always facing new challenges. You sometimes find yourself faced with aspects of your character or personality that you didn't know were there: you develop all the time. The fact that you're moving to a new environment every time means that you have to adjust, and draw upon your own resources to do so. So it strengthens you as you go along.

'Of course the same kind of thing may happen if you remain in your own home town, but the challenges are so much more numerous when you're moving around, that you're constantly forced to renew yourself. It isn't always easy, but I have found it almost always positive in the end. I like this sort of challenge.

'Moving is always a shock to the system and to the family. It does bring certain strains. And the environment to which you move is very important. It can make a posting pleasant or can mar it terribly, but this is external. It may orient your attitude this way or that way, but by itself, I don't believe that it can really alter a person's deep self. The base, I think, remains the person, the character, the personality, the identity that makes each person himself or herself.

'There are dangers, sometimes that you do not foresee, and that may come from an environment that is too pleasant. Before coming to Brussels, we were in Montevideo. It was a very pleasant, easy way of life; I didn't have to face the challenge of learning a new language; my frame of reference was roughly the same as that of the people I met. But I found, eventually, that I was lulled by all this, and I began to let myself go. I went to the club to play tennis, to tea parties with the women; we spent all summer at the beach. And I found that my mind was not being stretched, that it was too relaxing. I didn't like it in the end, I felt it could be really dangerous for me.

'When we came to Brussels, I was delighted. For not only were there lots of external challenges, but there was also an expatriate community that was particularly active and positive. I started to feel alive again. I took a course in photography and I feel that this is now developing as a *métier*.

'On the other hand, because my husband's now got an important post in the embassy, I am called upon to entertain a lot. At first I didn't like it, because until now I have been under no real obligation to act as official hostess, and my husband's not at all demanding. But I now realize that it's going to be necessary to his career, and I have come to see it as another way of helping him.

'So you could say that for both of us moves have strengthened our relationship. But I think it was a strong relationship to start with. Each of us had a role to play that suited him or her and that helped the other, and when contingencies came, we had to adapt our lives to fit them in.

EG -
This bears out what we were saying earlier, that if each partner is basically fulfilled and autonomous, the marriage has a good chance to thrive. In your case, Maria, it had the added strength that you were complementary to each other to start with.

'If we can recap briefly, most of us seem to agree that a move emphasizes certain traits of a marriage or of individual personalities, that it can add external strains that are quite particular to a mobile way of life - in a nutshell, that it is not only an upheaval, but also a catalyst.

'Now another thing that seems evident but that we have not directly talked about is that almost every move, whatever the ultimate outcome, tends to polarize the husband and wife roles within a family. By that, I mean that because, in a lot of cases the wife can't work, she becomes the home and family caretaker, and her husband becomes the breadwinner. In the case of Maria, this was the structure of the relationship to start with, except that she always played a particularly active social role as - what was it you said, Maria? - a "forger of human contacts". Often, however, the spheres of work and home are more clearly marked in expatriate households, and curiously this holds true even when the woman has a job. There is less, or even no, sharing of household tasks, hardly any shared parenting of the children. And this is certainly due at least in part to mobility, which in most cases entails a promotion for the husband, more work, more money, a sense of social status that might make him reluctant to be seen to help with household matters, and, of course, extensive travelling. Now I'm aware that I'm making a gross generalization here, but the general polarization of household roles is something that the large majority of expatriate women we talked to have noticed.

Monica -
Oh, I've noticed it also, and it's something I deplore, because it increases the gap between a wife and a husband. In our own case, when we were living in the States and I was working, we were on an almost equal basis - I say "almost" because I wasn't earning as much money as Jerry did, but it didn't matter. It was quite a democratic household. We didn't have any children and there was a lot of task-sharing in our household. Jerry used to shop and vacuum-clean and he enjoyed cooking, which he did quite frequently. The moment we moved to England, however, things changed drastically. First I was at home all day (when I wasn't out looking for a job), then he became increasingly involved in his work, and, finally, I think his status as an up-and-coming young executive kind of went to his head. I resented all this but I felt morally incapable of asking him to do anything in the house because I was at home all day "doing nothing".

Judy -
This is exactly what happened to us as well, and I can see it happening all over expatriate communities everywhere. Of course you have countries where this kind of role polarization exists as a general cultural fact. But in Anglo-Saxon or Scandinavian countries, for instance, couples, especially youngish middle-class couples, started quite a while ago to move away from this kind of situation. So when we, for instance, moved to France, there was, as with your household, Monica, quite a lot of task-sharing in the house and out of it. But it's a direct, or semi-direct result of mobility that this sort of thing stops when you start living abroad and you return to a more traditional family style. In fact you realize, when you live in an international community, that this is the norm. In many ways it's as if you've been pushed back a quarter of a century in time. It's as if the women's movement had never happened.

EG -
What I found most difficult to accept was the sudden change our own move brought to the way we were bringing up our son. In Paris, both my husband and I played a very active part in his upbringing, right from the very beginning. Then it suddenly changed because my husband became increasingly involved in his work here and increasingly reluctant to spend his few leisure hours in being an active father - although I must admit he seems to do far more around the house than most men I know, both abroad and at home.

Esther -
The result however is that their lack of physical and emotional availability makes them feel like outsiders eventually. I think that one of the things that Steve resented during those years when he

was commuting from Paris to Brussels was that at times he felt redundant in his own home. The kids got used to not having him there most of the time, so it was me they told about whatever had happened at school.

'In fact, whether your husband is an international commuter like mine was, or whether he's just often absent as a lot of expatriate husbands are, the women end up feeling like single parents.

MJ -
Sociologists have a rather horrid term for that. The women are known as "isolated matriarchs"!

Esther -
That's what I was alright - an isolated matriarch, except it felt more like a young divorcee or widow at the time. I couldn't bear to think of the responsibility I had. It was mindboggling, especially if you haven't yet had a chance to build your own support network. You can't help feeling, "Oh God! What would happen to those kids if I fell under a bus? Who's going to fetch them from the school bus stop?" I had a vision of their standing there in the rain, while I was lying unconscious somewhere, with no one knowing of their existence, except their father who was three hundred kilometres away. Of course this got better as I began to make friends. I felt less threatened in my role as a single parent.

MJ -
Yes, this is very much where friends come in, eventually. They begin to replace your family. They become a real support network. I find that, when you live abroad, there's often an extra depth or solidarity in friendships, especially with other expatriates, because you know you have to depend on one another.

EG -
And this, of course, very much depends on where you live. Those of us who are living in Brussels or in Geneva are indeed very lucky, for a lot of support networks have been created by generations of expatriates and the cities are small enough for relationships to be sustained. If you were living as a foreigner in London, say, or Paris, I think you'd probably feel a lot more isolated, for both the size of the city and the pace of life would conspire against friendships and support networks developing quite so easily.

Polly -
Well, I didn't find any of those networks you're talking about when I was living in Geneva - but then perhaps I didn't know where to look. Eventually I did make some very good friends, but for a long

time I didn't have any. And I needed friends desperately, particularly when I got pregnant, which made me feel very vulnerable. I didn't want to talk to my husband. I felt he was already under considerable pressure from his work and I thought I really had to look after myself. I tried not to put my inadequacies, as I saw them, onto him. In fact I felt the need to conceal them because I felt I ought to be able to cope with these things. They were trivial really. What was not trivial was the fact that I had lost total confidence in my capacity to interact with the environment.

Antonia -
All the more so, I expect, because you were pregnant. Although I've been used to being in foreign places since I was a child, it was really only when I became pregnant that I felt desperately in need of the presence of my mother and my closest friends. It was a terribly isolating experience.

Judy -
Crucial moments in a person's life, like pregnancy, childbirth, accidents, illness, marital crises or whatever, always seem that much worse when you're living abroad, even if you have friends. They're these strange moments when, even if you really think you've outgrown your family back home, you revert, or regress, to a kind of primitive urge to be surrounded by them.

MJ -
I'd like for a moment to go back to the point Polly just made, which is central to a lot of women who live abroad and find it difficult to adapt - and that is the question of guilt. They feel they ought to be coping better with some of the problems of adjustment that confront them, and they feel guilty about their sense of inadequacy. They're ashamed of it and they can't express it. When this project about expatriate wives got under way and we started to interview women and organize group discussions, we were amazed by the number of women who said, "Just talking about how I have been feeling makes me feel so much better. And I don't feel so isolated anymore. I didn't realize so many women felt like me."

Judy -
There's a lot of guilt around anyway, whichever way you look at it, and it affects all family relationships. Men don't usually express it, but I know for a fact that many men who have dragged their wives and children after them feel a certain amount of guilt when they realize that moving may not be a bed of roses for the rest of their family.

'Most men, however, are on such a different wavelength that they really are not able to understand why their wives are not happy. They say "Just think of how much better off you are than if we were still at home - you don't have to work, I have a huge salary, we've a lovely big house, a maid or a cleaning woman who comes often, you're travelling all over the place, the children are growing up to be international, it's a wonderful experience for them - what more can you possibly want?" And of course, faced with this constant litany of advantages, how can women not feel guilty about their unhappiness or difficulties in coping? I'm not trying to lay all the guilt at the men's door, but I wish they could understand that there's perhaps more to the quality of life than material advantages.

Monica -
I'm with you all the way here. But in a sense I feel women can pull themselves together - they're adults after all. It's true that moves reveal things about your character that you didn't know were there - in my case, for instance, it showed me that I was far more passive than I ever imagined I was. Another woman in my situation might have got up and found work, and fought to survive in a much more energetic way.

'But I think that the greatest guilt of all is about the children, carting them about like luggage, breaking up their friendships, forcing them to change schools, bringing them up far from their own home.... and wondering all the time what the hell is going to happen to them when they grow up.

Judy -
Well, of course it's unsettling for kids to be brought up this way, especially if one moves around very frequently. But you know, I've always found children are much tougher than we parents think they are. It's our own guilt that expresses itself when we say, "How are they going to cope?" But in fact most of them seem to adapt better and faster than we think. The trouble is, that with all this travelling, you lose confidence. You lose confidence when you're uprooted and moved around - confidence in yourself and also confidence in your children. I always go home to England thinking that my boys are not going to be up to the level of my friends' children, who've been at home all the time. But of course that's not true at all. They're different, of course, because they've had more varied experiences and they've made extra efforts to adjust, but they're perfectly able to defend themselves among their peers.

Elvira -
I think so too, but I feel nevertheless that we must make special efforts to ensure that they have continuity in their lives. Of course we, as parents, keep them in touch with their own culture and their

own language. But quite early my husband and I decided that it was important for them to have continuity in the language and method they were schooled in, and since we could not always be sure to find a Spanish school in all the places we were posted to, we decided to send them, right from the beginning, to American schools. So they've always found it easy and straightforward.

'They've grown up with two basic languages Spanish and English, but they picked up other languages without any problem from the children they played with in our different postings. In Israel, for instance, they played with children who spoke Hebrew and got to know the language this way; the same thing happened in Germany and Portugal.

'The most positive thing about it is that I think my children have a wider and perhaps deeper culture than their contemporaries in Venezuela. And, of course, a wider vision of things in general. The problem, as I see it, is that despite all this they feel Venezuelan and part of them longs to go home and stay there and have friends who do not come and go. This, of course, becomes more marked now that they are adolescents. There are always problems then, but there will be those problems wherever they are, even in their own country. Generally, however, I find that very mobile children learn to develop more resources with which to construct their lives than children who have always stayed home, protected by their family and culture.

Antonia -
Don't they find that they lack really deep friendships because they, or their friends, are always on the move?

Elvira -
Yes, that is a problem, They tend to have acquaintances rather than friends.

Antonia -
I remember this happened to me as well. And the other children who were moving constantly never became really close to other kids. When they left, more often than not they wouldn't leave forwarding addresses. However, as I grew up, I made closer friendships. This need for close friends becomes so strong when you're a teenager that finally it overcomes your defences.

Monica -
Well, I worry constantly about my children. They are American, yet they were brought up in England, and now in Belgium, where we chose to put them in the International School, which is really American.

MJ -

Why did you choose to put them there rather than in one of the British schools here, where at least they would have had some continuity in the system and curriculum?

Monica -

I guess because we thought that someday we'd go back to the States, and so we wanted them to be prepared for that. As it is, they're Americans, and yet they're not. Americans do not think of them as Americans, they think of them as snooty little Britishers who're just claiming to be Americans. They don't share with Americans the "communality" (if this word exists) of being brought up in that country, the T.V., the ads, the movies, the culture that you absorb in the U.S. And I start to think sometimes, "What are we creating with these children who are, in the best sense international, but in the worst sense totally rootless?"

Esther -

I feel very strongly that our kids are prototypes, and, as with all kinds of prototypes there's an element of danger involved. I had a very hard fight with my husband over our children's education. It was fundamental for me to ensure that we spoke English with them at home. But Steve who's a great francophile wanted to speak French to them, and all the more so since they all go to French-language schools. Well I stood up for what I believed and fought over it every step of the way, and eventually won. So, having worked through that and established the linguistic structure we have in our family, I actually think we're bringing up a new breed of children - a first generation of Europeans. I don't really think any of us can predict what's going to happen later on with those children, but at the moment I feel confident that we're bringing up some interesting hybrids.

'Nevertheless, in the end, our basic feeling is that our children need roots and a sense of cultural identity, and both of us are very torn about whether to give them a good, solid English sense of identity or go on trying to cultivate this very strange breed of new Europeans. There are not enough Euro children to show us where and if they are going to fit and what sort of community they're going to work and live in. The real issue will come over their secondary education.

MJ -

We got my daughter, when she was still at the European School, to organize group discussions with some of the other teenagers there. The outcome was that the great marjority of them had a very strong sense of being Europeans, and part of a wider culture, while at the same time they acknowledged a sort of emotional attachment to their own individual culture. My daughter had great misgivings about going to a British university. She was afraid to find everyone extremely narrow-minded. And of course, some of the young people she met were that. But she managed to make a lot of good friends and she loved being there. Now she's going to spend a year at the Sorbonne. I think she really thinks of herself as a British European, whatever that may mean.

Monica -
I really envy you Europeans sometimes because you're working towards making a new world in which there's going to be a lot of communication and exchanges between nations. It's far more difficult for American expatriates in Europe. Because America itself is so self-contained and has to impose its culture on so many immigrants, this makes it a difficult culture to amalgamate with a European culture.

EG -
It's all going to take several generations to work out, but I don't think it's something one can avoid. There's an ever-increasing internationalization of culture. We're a truly mobile society in every sense. And there are more and more mixed marriages, not only within multi-cultural societies like the U.S., but also among people who are internationally mobile. And this raises an additional question, which is to know which culture will be given priority in the bringing up of children: the father's, the mother's or that of the country they're living in.

Antonia -
This is a question which we had to face when we decided to have a family. As you know, I'm American (although I feel a bit like a hybrid because I was brought up as an itinerant child), and my husband is Danish. Well, we've kind of opted for an outright internationalism, with our two cultures being presented as alternatives for our children to choose from. So far it has not seemed to present any problem. They go to the European School - we preferred this to the International School because that would have favoured American culture and we didn't want this to happen. We tend to speak English or French at home, but their Danish is pretty good since they spend all their summer holidays with their cousins in Denmark. At Christmas and on other holidays we celebrate in a mixture of styles. In fact I can say that we've evolved a kind of individual brand of family culture and traditions, and I think this is quite valid.

EG -
In fact it's not just our children who are prototypes, but us as well,

because we're the ones who must establish our own individual brand of portable roots and family traditions. My husband and I also have a mixed marriage - but really a very mixed one. When we came to Brussels it became obvious that as our son was growing up he needed more and more to know what he was, and he found it too complicated to relate to our different backgrounds, so, as he was, like his father, born in Paris, he chose to be French.

'Then one year by chance I found myself travelling from Italy with a very interesting woman who was a French psychoanalyst, and she asked me whether my husband and I ever discussed our childhood memories with our son. I said that we tended not to overmuch, because he had obviously been a bit confused when he was younger by the sort of Babel-like background we were confronting him with.

'She disagreed with this attitude and we had a most interesting discussion during which some of the questions I had been asking myself about expatriates and how to resolve the problem of roots and cultural identity, became clearer. This woman's idea was that, since it was imperative for people on the move to retain a feeling of belonging to some sort of social group somewhere and above all to pass this sense of belonging to their children, it was important to learn to live not with a traditional sense of place and roots, but with something more "portable", and fluid, and individual. Thus, she thought it important for us to present our child with an array of family memories, experiences and anecdotes into which he could dip as and when he felt like it. At first it would be a sort of handed-down tradition, but later, as he grew up, it would become his own heritage of family lore. We would give him a kind of data-bank, as it were, a family data-bank, which would provide him with a basis onto which he could then graft his own experiences and memories, and which would constitute his "roots".

'To her, you see, roots did not mean necessarily a sense of belonging to a country, or a town, or a community. It is more like an internal state, made up of the memory of commitments - to individuals, to many places, to lifestyles, to shared values. And once the notion of roots was accepted as an internal state, those roots could then become truly "portable", and be passed on to other generations as such.

Polly -
It is interesting, but, if you'll forgive me, you all sound so intellectual, as if bringing up kids happens in a vacuum. Whatever decisions are taken about the language they're going to be brought up in, their schooling, their family data-bank, or whatever, children

are basically nothing but the sounding-board of what's going on in the family - for better or for worse, and, in our case, I'm afraid it was for worse.

'I'm in Brussels on a visit after three years at home in England. Before that we had been living in Geneva for fifteen years. I've had to do a lot of thinking about moving after what happened in our family and I've come to a rather dismal conclusion about what it does to family relationships - if our story can in any way be called typical.

'I have to start at the beginning in order for you to understand. Well, you've gathered by now that my name's Polly. I'm 46 years old, British, married to a corporation lawyer, and we have two daughters. We only moved once, to Geneva - and that was plenty for me. I cannot for a minute visualize what a lifetime of moving from country to country would have done to us. I guess some people have a greater natural aptitude to adapt. Perhaps they are more flexible, or their needs for security are less gnawing than mine.

'Anyway.... When Tom and I married in London, he was working as a legal adviser within a multinational. I was working in the personnel department of another multinational. We both had good jobs, with decent salaries and quite a few responsibilities. And the joke of it was that, in my capacity as a personnel executive, I was sending people to live abroad!

'Tom and I were roughly equal in terms of grades and salaries, we didn't have any children, and everything seemed very democratic in our household. I mean there was no real difference in our roles. About a year after we were married, Tom was offered a job with another corporation in Geneva. And although the salary he was offered was quite a large one, it didn't make up for the loss of mine. But this didn't matter a bit at the time. It all seemed like a fantastic adventure, and that's how we approached it. I never hesitated about breaking up my career - I was pretty self-confident about my ability to get myself a good job when and if I wanted to work after we'd settled in.

'However, it didn't feel a bit like an adventure when we actually got to Geneva. I thought the place smug, bourgeois, and full of bland, middle-class executives and their wives who were leading a dull, though seemingly gilded international life. I was terribly disappointed that it was not as exciting as I thought it was going to be.

'What really floored me, however, was the inadequacy of my own reaction. I found it quite terrible to be on my own. And on my own I was practically all the time, for from the moment we got there, Tom was swallowed up by his job. That was something else I hadn't foreseen. Right from the start our stay in Geneva was coloured by a sense of doom. The move showed me that I had no personal resources, that I had until then relied totally on the environment, on my friends and on the people I worked with to give me a sense of who I was. In Geneva, suddenly, I no longer knew who I was. I was terribly intimidated by everything in a way I'd never thought it possible at home.

'When we'd first arrived, a woman from Tom's office took me round the supermarket, but when I tried to go on my own, I got lost. I couldn't find my way home. I wandered around for two hours with this great big bag of shopping. I couldn't speak enough French to follow the instructions of the people who tried to help me. I felt like a child. And another time I tried to get on a bus the wrong end and everybody shouted at me and laughed. I felt really humiliated. I, the independent executive, who'd sent countless people abroad without a flicker of doubt that they would all adapt perfectly, found myself totally unable to cope. It took me two full years before I could decide that life in Geneva was not totally a nightmare.

'I did try to get a job, but I must say I didn't try very hard. All the jobs that were offered to me seemed demotions. I was too proud, not flexible enough. Looking back I now see that I should have taken anything, anything to get some of my self-respect back. But at the time I felt, "Why the hell should I?" I had virtually been in charge of the personnel department of a huge firm and now in the jobs I was offered I would have had to type my own letters. Looking back, I am surprised by my lethargy.

Monica -
I really empathize with you there. I also felt that awful, paralyzing lethargy, that I just couldn't understand or really see at the time and that in retrospect seems so surprising. It's as if you become a different person.

Polly -
In a sense you do become a different person. Anyway there was also the feeling that this was a good moment to start a family. I was 28, no spring chicken, and there was nothing in the way of starting to have children. I did become pregnant after six months in Geneva.

'My relationship with my husband, now that I was no longer working, was difficult. As I said earlier in the discussion, he was under a certain amount of pressure at work and I didn't want to burden him with my inadequacies. In fact I was terribly ashamed of them. But I couldn't help looking unhappy and moaning at times, and he didn't like this change of role from the confident, active career woman he'd married.

'It wasn't just a problem of loneliness, it was a problem of incompatibility as well. I did get to meet a few expatriate women, but they were an alien breed to me, and I simply didn't want to be one of them. They were heavily into coffee mornings, tennis and golf, and all they could talk about was that, and company policies, children and househelp. They all seemed to be having a whale of a time, and I felt very out of place.

'Having a baby seemed to be a good thing, a positive thing. In fact it turned out to be an absolute disaster, and we eventually paid the price for that.

'We lived on the sixth floor of quite a grand block of flats. There were no other young families there and the only person I ever spoke to was the concierge. She would peek into the pram and say hello, and that was it. If I didn't go out to one of those dreadful coffee mornings, I wouldn't speak to anybody all day until Tom came home. What had appeared like a good solution - I mean, having a child - turned out not to be one at all. Putting that kind of investment into children is wrong.

'At that time in Geneva there wasn't any kind of playgroup such as there existed in England - or if there was, I was quite unaware of it. (Knowing now how clueless I was about facilities there for years, it wouldn't surprise me to hear that there were playgroups and that somehow I did not get to know about them.) Anyway I eventually heard of a playgroup that was being started by Anglo-Saxon women and I plucked up enough courage to go to one of the initial meetings, and one thing led to another, and I started to play an active part in the setting up of an English-language playgroup in Geneva. It was my salvation. Suddenly I felt I was in the land of the living. After four years, I had gathered up enough self-confidence to start operating commercially in bigger premises.

'I had another daughter just as I was getting going, and this time the experience was alright. I attribute the difference in my daughters' personalities to the different circumstances surrounding their births and early infancy. It seems quite obvious to me that all the problems we had later stemmed originally from the fact that I was absolutely distraught and in a state of depression when my first daughter was born and in her early childhood.

'Then Tom's company decided that they wanted to transfer us to the United States. Originally our stay in Geneva was to be for five years. I'd always known that, but nevertheless this decision felt as if it was coming out of the blue. I began to feel terribly insecure while negotiations were going on. I put up a fight, there were terrible repercussions within the family, rows and arguments, and our elder daughter began to exhibit symptoms of stress. I also realized that our marriage was by then in a very bad state. What Tom wanted out of it, what he expected from life and from me, were completely different to what I wanted from life and what I was prepared to give.

'Through a series of events, the American post fell through and I started to make efforts to improve our marital relationship. It wasn't successful basically, I think, because, despite my attempts at expressing my feelings, Tom wasn't really aware that there was anything wrong. But our elder daughter continued to be in distress and the problems increased all around.

'Two years after that Tom was offered a very important post with his own firm, in London. It was in fact a huge promotion. That put me in an awful quandary. In my head I'd always said that I'd refuse to be lugged around anywhere except to go home. I thought, "Now I'm in a spot, I can't refuse to go." It was a disaster for me, for by then I'd not only got used to life in Geneva, but I had actually come to like it. I had my job, my circle of friends, my commitments. It had started to feel a bit like home. This move back to England seemed suddenly like the end of the world to me. I didn't deal at all well with it. I can remember going around for a long time in a state of acute grief.

'The company gave Tom three weeks to decide - only it felt like ten minutes. He just moved out with his briefcase, and we followed in our own good time. But in the time we stayed behind in Geneva, our elder daughter got worse. She developed a school phobia. She was only ten. She couldn't or wouldn't say what was wrong, but she would not go to school at all. We'd been seeing a psychotherapist for about a year because of problems that had come up around the time of the proposal to go to the States. She advised me that my daughter should go to school no matter what, and the school must put up with whatever happened. So for a whole term I had to beat her up and drag her to school and drag her back again, and all the time in between she would sit and sob in the classroom all day. It was terrible - terrible for everybody. Then, in January, after Tom had been back in England a few months, it all stopped. I can only assume that she expected that we were in Geneva to stay, and that Tom was back in Britain, and that never the twain would meet.

'She had a real shock, however, when we moved in April. We'd bought a house in Kent, and I realized, just as we moved into it that it would be a disaster for me - for all of us. I just *knew* it, and that's how it turned out to be. I was so resentful that it couldn't possible have turned out differently.

'I found life in the village very hard. All the women there were into voluntary activities, and I decided not to get involved in any of these because I was adamant about getting back to work. While I was looking for a job I started getting involved in women's groups, and, what with Tom away in London all week, the children felt neither of us was ever there. I think they began to feel that none of my activities had anything to do with them and with our home, and they seemed to get anxious about my being involved with women of another age group and lifestyle. I think everyone felt threatened, but at the time I didn't realize that. I found the women's groups supportive, but in fact their support only fanned my resentment further.

'Then problems started again with our eldest child. Once again she refused to go to school. And here we made a big mistake: we decided to change her from the local comprehensive school to a private grammar, which was a smaller and quieter school.

'Before going to her new school, Emma decided that she was overweight and should lose some weight. She became obsessive about jogging. She used to run around the house for hours. Then, when she joined the new school her school phobia got worse and she eventually got expelled. By then we were really in serious trouble. We asked the psychiatric department of the local hospital for help. We told her she could choose any school she wanted, and she chose a progressive school not too far from where we lived. But once that line of action was shut she went back to her obsession with losing weight. This time she just starved herself.

'Her anorexia eventually became so severe that she was admitted as an emergency to the adolescent unit of the local psychiatric hospital and was there for ten months. But they were not able to cope with her problems. She was referred to the Maudsley in London and two years ago they started family therapy. It was dreadful.

'The upshot of it was that for a year, Emma and I were virtually prisoners in our house. We had to forcefeed her, we had to prevent her from going out to buy laxatives, and the only way to do that was to lock both her and me in the house. I used to keep my keys and money in my trouser pockets all the time, otherwise she would steal both. She actually climbed out of a window once when Tom was at home "babysitting", walked all the way to the next village (for they all knew her in our village), bought her laxatives, walked back and climbed back again, without anyone noticing. She couldn't stand the flesh on her legs, so she would stab her legs all over with biros. We were at our wits' end, and the Maudsley declared we were too rigid a family.

MJ -
Do you think all your troubles were the result of your move to Geneva and your eventual move back home?

Polly -
Yes, I do. I think that had we remained in Britain all these years ago, I would never have been faced with this aspect of my character which is that I am extremely dependent on my environment and my work to give me self-confidence and a sense of who I am; that I am not personally resourceful. Both Tom and I are fairly needy people and we tend not to support each other. We get what we need from outside the family, but as a family we are not particularly supportive of each other. This obviously has affected Emma from the start. Of all of us the second child seems to have been least affected by all these dramas - I suppose it's a question of inborn character as well.

'I guess that what happened to Emma was her way of punishing us for making her (though of course we did not mean to) the sounding-board of our own inadequacies and unhappiness, and for subjecting her to the insecurity of the prospect of other moves. She has identified two main areas in which she can injure her parents: one is education, because we both made a terrific investment in her education, as she is a very bright girl. I had her down in my own mind for Oxford and Cambridge as soon as she was born. So she knew exactly where to strike, and she had a powerful tool. The other, of course, is her health, which strikes at our vitals and makes us feel desperately guilty.

'Whenever problems came up with her, they were nearly always triggered off by an impending move, and the insecurity of what was going to happen to Mummy and Daddy and the children. Even though in Geneva she had been saying she was not happy there, it was in a sense the devil she knew, and she felt another place might be even worse, so she responded even more wildly. Anorexia, drug addiction, alcoholism - all these things go hand in hand, until she can be happier and face life without these "magic" solutions to life's problems. She's at terrific risk all the time, and this crucifies me.

'I don't feel at home in Britain. There is nothing there that is home. But where and what is "home" anyway? I suppose, at a pinch, it might be Geneva. It's where my children grew up and where I eventually made a network of friends who care about me. And yet, when Tom suggested that we should move back to Geneva, I said no, and I keep on saying no. His company, who wanted to move us again, were very displeased, although they knew the difficulties we had with Emma, because when we were forcefeeding her Tom had to stay at home in the mornings, as I couldn't manage on my own. But he feels, quite rightly I suppose, that you can't be working for a multinational and refuse a transfer. He doesn't want to call a halt to his career, not even for our sake. He wants to continue to have a challenging life at work. So now they're sending him, by himself, to the States for a year's exchange, and I shall stay here with the children. I don't look forward to single parenting, especially with the present situation, but I don't see what else I can do.

'I've discovered that I need continuity. I need things to grow slowly. After all these years, it only actually became clear to me last year. Although I tend to be quick in doing things, my natural rhythm is actually very slow, and I like to let things grow naturally. I need to move slowly from one thing to another and let it all flower. I do feel I was hacked out of the soil by these two moves and I was put down brutally, but I need time to let the roots flow out and unwind again to begin to feel firmly established.

'I know a lot of women manage this moving business. They take it in their stride, even though it is usually at some cost to themselves. It's important to have some support structure from the start. Some of the American women I met I found marvellous in their capacity to go from the American Women's Club in Rome to the A.W.C. in Amsterdam, to the A.W.C. in Timbuctoo. They seem to glide around the world almost painlessly because they have this support structure and they are all in the same boat together and they know how to protect themselves by all flocking together and not allowing the alien environment to phase them out.

'I felt all along that if I'd been more of a traditional person, I mean the sort of person I thought I was when I gave up my job to follow Tom to Switzerland - this would have been a happier experience for all of us and we would have managed the moves much better. It all depends on the mother, you see, and if the mother goes under, then everyone else in the family does too.

'Emma says her difficulties really started when I joined a rather active and outspoken women's group in Geneva. This was after my mother had died, and I had started to think "My God, I must see to it that I don't end up like her." Joining the women's group was an attempt to sort things out. Until then my whole life had been wrapped up in the family, but because I am not a traditional person at heart, I made a hash of it.

'So you see, had I remained in London, continued to be a career woman, and had children, a support structure - everything that my own generation of friends manage over there, I would not have had to face certain aspects of myself, which were revealed by the moves. And we would not be where we are today.'

3

Escape from the Doll's House

'Caroline,' demanded Miss Keeler abruptly, 'don't you wish
you had a profession, a trade?'

'I wish it fifty times a day. As it is, I often wonder what I came
into the world for. I long to have something absorbing and
compulsory to fill my head and hands, and to occupy my
thoughts.'

'Can labour alone make a human being happy?'

'No: but it can give varieties of pain and prevent us from
breaking our heart with a single master-torture.'

Charlotte Brontë,
Shirley, London, 1849

*This is part of a group discussion that took place in March 1986 in
Brussels. The women who participated were Joanna, 46, British;
Renate, 36, German; Britt, 39, Norwegian; Mary, 36, Irish; Anna, 49,
Danish and Faith, 30, American.*

MJ -
This evening I'd like us to concentrate on a subject that, from the
evidence we've had so far, is one about which a lot of women feel
very strongly - and that is the subject of work.

'We know, from the questionnaires women sent back, from what
they said in interviews and group discussions, as well as from
employers we interviewed, that it is a major issue in mobility.

'Many of the women who've been in touch with us have expressed
strong feelings of loss and frustration at not being able to work
abroad. I've made a short list of some of their remarks drawn from
their questionnaires, and I'll just quote a few of them:

'A Burmese economist, living in Rome, writes: "I feel useless, my
talent wasted and I am sometimes frustrated and depressed."
An American, living in Spain, says: "I feel powerless, helpless, extremely unhappy, resentful, purposeless; it is unrewarding and a
waste of life." Another describes herself as "frustrated and angry
with myself for being intimidated by the situation". And the list
goes on and on in this vein.

'Employers too have told us that, increasingly, the most important
obstacle to a professional man accepting a post abroad is that his
wife does not want to give up her career or job, irrespective of
whether or not his increased salary will make up for the loss of her
salary. So, for the employers too, the question of expatriate wives'
work is very important.

'None of this is surprising when you set expatriate women within
the context of what women generally in the Western world have
come to expect. Within the last twenty to thirty years, whatever the
gains and losses of the women's movement, there is no doubt that
there has been an enormous change in relation to women having
jobs and careers. The social recognition of having a professional
activity, financial independence, and the autonomy and fulfilment
that derive from it, are all part of what women have come to expect
from life.

'I think I should say, however, that the feelings of frustration I have
been talking about are not shared by all the women who have been
in touch with us. Many were quite happy not to be working, when

previously they had been employed; others, who had not been working at home saw no reason to start working abroad. Nevertheless, as I said before, the subject of work does arouse strong feelings among a large number of expatriate women, and this is why we think it would be interesting to concentrate on this subject tonight.

Joanna -
By "work", you seem to be meaning remunerated work rather than any occupation outside housework, such as voluntary work and so on.

MJ -
Yes, that's what I meant really - a job or career. We'll probably find, as we go along, that the boundaries between voluntary or unpaid creative work and remunerated work are sometimes blurred. But rather than go on about it, I'd like each of you in turn to tell us about yourself, what your professional experience was prior to living abroad and how being an expatriate has affected that aspect of your life. Renate, would you like to start the ball rolling?

Renate -
I am German, 36 years old, married to a journalist, and we have no children. I am very new to Brussels - we have only been here eight months. This is our first international move, but I believe it is going to be the first of many because my husband's been made a foreign correspondent.

'I too was a journalist in Germany, and I'm still working as a journalist here, except that it is in a freelance capacity and I am doing it at a distance. I find it's quite different from working for a particular newspaper.

EG -
Different in what way?

Renate -
Well, you're really on your own as a freelancer. You're no longer part of a team, or a newspaper. People don't really know you. You feel insecure. Of course, I hope this will change in time, but in Germany I was quite well-known in journalistic circles.

'I worked in Düsseldorf for eleven years, then my husband was moved to Cologne. In Düsseldorf I had been part of the art department of a newspaper, but in Cologne I started to get very involved in the theatre and became a theatre critic. This is what people came to know me as. I had my own column. Coming here was a shock, because here I am nobody. It's a bore for people to hear me say that in Germany I was a theatre critic, so I don't say it much.

'And so people here only know me as the woman who entertains her husband's colleagues and cooks a delicious goose, or whatever. Being a good cook is not the kind of attention I am interested in attracting.

'I'd like to say here, right at the beginning of this discussion, that for me, the biggest thing about moving to Brussels was this sudden drop into anonymity and nothingness. I had felt confident and capable in my job, and when I had that pulled out from under me, I felt worthless, unproductive, incompetent and without skills. I know it's probably just a phase I am going through, but it is unpleasant and depressing.

Britt -
It's true that without professional recognition we're nobody really. Just an appendage: so-and-so's wife, or so-and-so's mother.

MJ -
Joanna, is this how you feel about work and professional recognition as well?

Joanna -
To some extent, though for me it wasn't quite so obvious or so clear-cut. I was quite happy being a wife and mother for a while, then I started to want to extend myself in another direction as well as remaining a wife and mother.

'I originally trained as a social worker in Britain but never actually used my training, because no sooner had I finished than my fiancé, who was in the Foreign Office, was given a posting abroad, and we got married right away and went to live in Singapore.

EG -
Were you able to work at all during your years as a diplomat's wife?

Joanna -
No. You see my children were born pretty soon after we went abroad and, what with the pressures of being a diplomatic wife, it would have been difficult. Eventually, after several postings - to other places in the Far East, then to Rome - my husband applied for a job at the Commission when Britain joined the E.C. and we came to Brussels in 1973. And I found that things were very different as a non-diplomat's wife.

MJ -
Different in what way?

Joanna -
I won't go into it here because we're talking about work, but there
is a vast difference. You're freer to make your own choices about
your life, for one thing.

'Anyway, to get back to our move to Brussels, after a while I got
involved with the Help Line*. When I look at my diaries now I realize
what an important part this played in my life. But I always felt
slightly that I was just playing at social work. I would have liked to
go back to what I had originally trained for, but of course at that
time my qualifications were not recognized in Belgium. I hesitated
to do a course in French, for, although my French is good enough
to do the actual course in, I didn't think that it could stand up to
counselling or social work, for this is a field in which language is
very important. You have to really catch the nuances of what
people are trying to say.

'I very much wanted, at that point in my life, with the children
growing up, to do something constructive. I'd enjoyed a lot of my
life so far - the travelling, the different places - but I felt as if I were
playing at things. Then one day a friend who knew me well
suggested that I might make a good lawyer. I remember sitting with
her on my terrace and saying: "Oh.... That's not a bad idea!"

'However I couldn't at first see what openings there could be. But
the longer I worked on the Help Line, the more it became clear that
there was a need in Brussels for a British lawyer specializing in
family law. People were constantly asking for help with legal
matters to do with matrimonial problems in a foreign land. Here at
last was something solid, something that would give me some sort
of security and be constructive. You never know what's going to
happen in life: you may be widowed or deserted, too old to find work
and with no children at home. I suppose my voluntary work had
exposed me to those possibilities. I wanted some independence,
not from the family, but more for my long-term security and for the
sake of doing something in my own right. So, to cut a long story
short, I managed to train as a British sollicitor through a correspondence course. I had to do my articles in the UK, which wasn't
easy for the family, and I now work in Brussels as a lawyer
specializing in family affairs.

MJ -
What about you, Britt?

*A telephone service for advice and psychological help, run by voluntary
workers and created by the Community Help Service in Brussels.

Britt -
Well, I'm 39, Norwegian and my husband's American. He works for
an American company, and we have two children aged eight and
ten. You find me in a state of panic and confusion because we've
just heard that my husband's been moved to the South of France.

'The reason I'm so upset is that I've just finished a degree in
Business Studies and I was ready to go and get a job and, all of a
sudden, everything has to be put aside once again for the umpteenth
time. We've moved so many times around the world. At some point,
like you, Joanna, I did some voluntary work - mine was with a
Norwegian charity organizing the exchange of craftwork with
people from Third-World countries. But I decided voluntary work
was not the answer for me. I was ready to leave Dick - my husband
- at that point and go anywhere I could get a training. But just then
we were told we had to go to Brussels, and I was very glad, because
I knew there was an American University there, and that I could get
a training at last and look for a job. Then, suddenly, after two and
a half years, we're going somewhere else again where there isn't any
multinational company that I might get a job with.

'When I think of moving it sends a shudder through me because
this is what I've been doing all my married life, and this is what my
C.V. reflects. And you cheat and try to fix your C.V. in blocks so that
people won't notice right away that you've never been anywhere
long enough, but it just isn't any good. It works against you.

'Recently, when I went down to Nice to visit my kids' future schools,
what I got thrown in my face by the principals - both women and
men - was: "Oh, you won't mind driving the kids to school for half
an hour in the morning and in the evening, will you?" I thought I
was past that years ago, and all of a sudden I am being put back
into a role where I can't look for any serious job because two hours
of my time each day are being spent driving my kids to and from
school. I feel that's an enormous step backwards. It's a shock to
realize that this is how my time is being considered by others.

'You begin to think that it was just a joke that you ever went to
university at all. It was something to occupy your time. It was silly
to even think it could be more. The most important thing is that the
family should be settled.

'It always takes everybody a certain amount of time to get going -
at least six months. Then, as soon as you get started you don't have
time to fulfill what you've started. You don't ever move up the
ladder because it's time to go to the next place and there the
circumstances won't be the same. So you change your plans, and

you change your idea of a career depending on who you meet. And after a while you get tired of making all this effort. And you start blaming yourself, saying "You can't ever pull anything together", and "What's wrong with you, you've let all these years get the best of you and you didn't do anything with them."

EG -
I think Britt's just voiced something we have heard frequently in the last few months from women whose husbands are forced by their profession to move a lot - as opposed to women who move abroad once or for a long period of time. It's a mixture of discouragement and anger, which often turns to self-blame.

Britt -
Yes, it's easier - and safer - don't you think, to blame yourself. It would destroy a marriage eventually if you blamed it all on your husband. I did nearly leave Dick once, but I realize that it's not his fault really. I don't even get angry - I get depressed, fed up with the situation.

MJ -
Mary, you're in that position too, given your husband's profession. How do you feel about it?

Mary -
I'm 36 and come from Dublin. I'm a teacher and my husband's in the Irish Diplomatic Service. We have two children. I can certainly sympathize with what Britt's just said. But I can also to some extent sympathize with the employer's point of view. I know of a lot of people who've been turned down for jobs while being told that they were definitely the best person for the job - but since they could not guarantee that they would be working for a certain amount of time, they simply could not have the job. It's different in America, of course: mobility is such a widespread thing that it's taken for granted. People in middle or top management just move from one job to the other. Here in Europe it's still looked upon in a very negative way.

EG -
You've moved a lot in the last few years. I know you've got a job here in Brussels, but have you always been able to find work wherever your husband was posted?

Mary -
Well, yes, in one way or another. First because I can never exist without some kind of a job - it's as essential as oxygen to me so I do everything, but everything, in my power to get something.

Second, because since I trained as a teacher, this is always something I can fall back upon - even though I haven't always worked as a teacher.

MJ -
Did you know you were going to be moving around when you married?

Mary -
Yes, I knew perfectly well what was in store for me when I married Kevin because he already was in the Irish Diplomatic Service. I had been teaching in Dublin and I'd known him for a year and a half, when he was told he was going to be sent to New York. He asked me to marry him and we were married within a week. I was young and full of enthusiasm and energy, and the world was my oyster. I didn't think of difficulties - I didn't see difficulties. At the grand old age of 25 I had two degrees and a post-graduate qualification. Education has been the absorbing interest in my life so far. I saw Kevin's posting as a temporary break, a kind of enforced sabbatical. Meanwhile there was this exciting life ahead of me, and I simply rolled along.

'We landed in New York on the 21st of July 1972, and I bought *The New York Times* on the way from the airport. I like to get to grips with a place through its local newspaper, and I looked at the job ads straightaway. The next day, which was a Saturday, I rang up one number, which was for an ad for Westinghouse, and arranged for an interview on the Monday at 10.30.

'It was about a project to convert a high school learning programme to a computer linear programme. Westinghouse's attitude was to ask me in effect: "How good are you?" I realized that if I was going to be shy I'd be lost, so I told them just how good I was and they said: "Can you start now?"

'In all our moves it was this attitude that saved me. But Geneva was very much an employment black spot in my life. The Swiss are particularly difficult, what with *carte de séjour* and work permit and all that. I got round it by accepting unpaid work and worked at the school in our local commune.

'Later, when we got to Brussels, it was much easier. I registered for a course at the Open University and applied for a job at St John's school, and I was working the next day.

'Something I find very important is that no matter what I'm doing, I think in blocks of four years - which is the average length of our postings.

EG -

So if you were to move again tomorrow, it wouldn't bother you too much?

Mary -

It would hardly bother me at all. Believe me, I'm never held up for very long. If we were told we had to go to Moscow in the morning, I wouldn't be the least bit upset. I would just go, but before I got on the plane I would make four or five phone calls to say, "I'm coming and is there anything I can do?"

MJ -

How did you get around the fact that the diplomatic services of a lot of countries frown upon their diplomats' wives working, or even forbid it altogether?

Mary -

We're very lucky in the Irish Diplomatic Service: wives can work as long as the work doesn't embarrass our government.

EG -

This is also the case for the Danish Diplomatic Service, is it not, Anna? In fact I believe it is one of the few foreign services that actually go out of their way to help their diplomats' wives find work.

Anna -

Yes, you're quite right. The Ministry for Foreign Affairs in Denmark is a very flexible and human organization. It's very common, for instance, that people working for Foreign Affairs are married to civil servants in other ministries, so between the different ministries they can push to get wives jobs.

MJ -

And have you always been able to find work wherever your husband was posted?

Anna -

Yes, although it was not always remunerated work. I realize, as I listen to all your stories, that although I seem to have had a lot of different experiences, there's nevertheless a continuity to my life. When I was quite young I went for an interview to a training college for midwives and they asked me why I wanted to become a midwife. I said it was because I wanted to work with women. They were surprised: most applicants say it's because they want to work with babies. So you see, what's given my life continuity is my interest in the women's cause.

MJ -
Did you become a midwife, then?

Anna -
Yes, and I worked as a midwife in Copenhagen for many years. Then my husband started on his round of postings and we moved, first to Brussels - where I had my two children - then back to Copenhagen, to Paris, back to Denmark, to Brussels again and now, once more, to Paris.

'On the first posting in Paris I worked in a voluntary capacity, but it was very important to me. I had quite a mission. It was the period - in 1967 - when they were thinking about the planning of an abortion law in France. I had contacts with the French Family Planning Association, doctors and lawyers whom I had met in international meetings in Copenhagen and elsewhere. So for three years I helped them in planning and writing up a French Abortion Law project, by giving them detailed explanations about the development of the four different Danish abortion laws over the years and telling them about the abortion laws of other countries and about those countries that do not recognize it. Also in Paris I accompanied a French gynaecologist in his work in a hospital.

'I felt that although I was not being paid for my work, it was very worthwhile. After all it was not possible to work officially at that time since Denmark was not yet in the European Community. I felt that way I was keeping in touch with my profession and I was of use.

MJ -
What did you do after Paris?

Anna -
We went back to Denmark for five years and I had a chance to work on a number of exciting projects. I was hired by the Ministry of Foreign Affairs to work on the Danish contribution to the United Nations International Population Year and Conference in Bucharest, so I did that for a year and a half. It gave me experience in administration and in dealing with the intermediary world between the practical world and public policy. Then, when I finished that we went into all the preparations for the United Nations Women's Year Conference which was to be held in Mexico. There were other projects as well, then we left Denmark to go to Brussels.

EG -
And how did you feel about that?

Anna -

I must say it's all a question of who you are. If you're the kind of person who wants to do new and exciting things, you may not really care if you have job security. I was always willing to take the chance. If I had been one of those who follow a career and want to do the same thing for years, I would probably have decided to stay in Copenhagen. There is no pressure from the Danish Diplomatic Service for wives to follow their husbands at all costs. A lot of Danish women decide to stay at home either because of their work or simply because they want to.

MJ -

Were you able to work in Brussels?

Anna -

Again, it all depends on what you call "work". As you yourself said, at the beginning of the discussion, the boundaries are often blurred.

'In Brussels I got very involved with the women's movement, which is perhaps an obvious thing to do when you're in a place where you meet women from so many different countries and you see the differences in their conditions. I became involved in the formation of the Women's European Action group - this was a pressure group that came together as a result of the first direct European elections. And from this came C.R.E.W., the Centre for Research on European Women. It's a cooperative, and I'm one of the founding members. I wasn't paid: we could only afford two people's salaries and of course, being a founding member, I couldn't be on the pay roll in these circumstances. I would actually have loved to have been paid. That is a very personal question indeed, and a lot depends on the attitude of your husband. And, of course, it was quite tricky in my case, because I was doing a lot of counselling with women, telling them that being economically independent is the most important thing in the world. Of course I can say that whenever we were in Denmark I was being paid for what I did. But in a sense I've never stopped working, so I'm not really contradicting my own preaching. So, to get back to your question, yes, I did work in Brussels, at least in my own definition of the word.

EG -

There is always a very interesting debate among expatriate wives about paid and voluntary work, and about the economic dependence which living abroad sometimes forces on women. But perhaps before we come to that we should hear what Faith has to say about her own experience.

Faith -

I don't know where to start.... I'm American, just thirty, my husband's a businessman and we have three kids. I think I should say, right from the beginning that, of all the women who are here tonight, I am perhaps the only one who's happy doing nothing. I don't mean that I don't do anything with my life - but simply that I'm enjoying being a homemaker and mother full-time for a while.

MJ -

Did you work when you were in the States?

Faith -

Yes, I've always worked full-time basically, with sporadic times of staying at home when my children were babies. When I left high school I went to work in the business area, then in telecommunications, then in accounting, and, by the time I left I was doing the paperwork for training activities, which was very fulfilling - probably the most challenging work I've ever done.

'I was very happy working. I enjoy working, it makes me feel good. I hardly ever stayed home in the States. All my relationships, apart from the family, were basically with people from work.

'I was very excited about coming to Europe. I guess a lot of Americans feel that way. It's a glamorous place to be. I've been here a year and I've had really good experiences. We're supposed to be here for one more year, but who knows, it may be longer. The company my husband works for has a stranglehold on our lives. They have all this power over where I'm going to be, and you can't live just waiting to hear where you're going next or whether you're staying. If I had a job here I'd worry more, but as I'm a homemaker now, I don't think about it much. I think, "I'll just live". If I were really unhappy, however, I'd go back, I'd make my opinion known.

Britt -

After having earned your own living in the States, don't you feel threatened by financial dependence?

Faith -

Not really. At least not right now. There is an expectation between ourselves - between my husband and me and between our group of friends that, of course, we will both be employed and, of course, we will both contribute to the running of the household. We've been sharing so much until now. Even in the States our friends are surprised about our roles in the household being so equal. We'll have a party and they'll say to me, "That was a great dinner." And I'll say, "Thank you, Bill made it."

'I worked all the time in the States. I am basically a feminist - I
believe very strongly in women, I think they have a lot of force, they
can shape things. I never saw myself as a homemaker. I didn't look
down on it, but I could never see myself in that role. And now it has
become reality. It hit me only the other day. I went out and bought
a new tablecloth, and it suddenly hit me that I'm really a homemaker now. I tried to do something different for my family and they
noticed it; they appreciated it. And that was what hit me - that
homemakers have their place. Now I've really seen what it's like to
stay at home and look after your family. And they appreciate it.

Britt -
You'd better be careful - they'll keep you there.

Joanna -
You're all laughing, but actually that's always a very real danger.
I found it really difficult, when I was working at home, to get the
family organized and, above all, to get them to accept that I was
really working and not there at their beck and call.

Anna -
Yes, you have to get yourself an "alibi" they'll understand, or else
go to an office. It is always difficult for women who work from home,
whether they are living abroad or in their own country. But it is
even more difficult when you're living abroad because the family
makes so many more demands on you.

Britt -
This is one of the things that terrify me about going to Nice. There
are going to be so many demands made on me that I'll have no time
or energy left to cope with job-hunting. I'm going to have to deal
with Dick adjusting to a new job, with the children adjusting to new
schools and not having their friends around. What's more, they
don't speak French (we live in a Flemish neighbourhood here and
they've been going to a Dutch-language school), so there will have
to be a great deal of support on my part and a constant physical
presence too. And after all these years, I'm just fed up with the
endless supporting role I have to play.

EG -
I'm afraid that this is the almost inevitable role that women play in
a move. If there's one thing that the women we've talked to so far
have been virtually unanimous about, it's that the woman's role in
any move is a crucial one. We've got a list here of how they described
this role. There was a question about it in our questionnaire, if you
remember.... Here we are - at random: "pivot", "anchor", "manager",
"mainstay and prop", "backbone", "assimilator of information",

"social integrator", "sacrificial lamb", "organizer", "smoother of the path", "stabilizer", "the Drudge", "mother, maid, nanny and sergeant", "a piece of the world left behind", "cement", "wheelbarrow", and so on. Only very occasionally do you get less strongly defined descriptions of the role they feel they have played. There's one I particularly like, from an American who's been travelling too long: "I came. I cope. I try not to bitch."

Britt -
You're all laughing again, but I assure you, it's dramatic. And it does go on and on, if you're one of those families that move constantly, because, unless you stay in one place long enough, your kids don't get the chance to make their own links. So you have to go on doing a lot of things for them which you wouldn't have to do if you were at home.

Mary -
Oh, children are much tougher than you think. They usually adapt remarkably quickly. Don't you think that if you really wanted to find work, you'd get something? Don't you think this is a kind of excuse that some women give themselves? It's sometimes an alibi for not working.

MJ -
Hang on a minute - you must admit that there are very concrete obstacles to expatriate wives getting jobs. Many women can't work abroad because they don't speak the language of their host country, or because they're not allowed to legally - either because they need a work permit and these are difficult to obtain in many countries especially with the present state of unemployment, or because their husbands' employers veto it. As you know, a lot of diplomatic services won't allow their people's wives to do any remunerated work - just "acceptable" voluntary activities and, of course, entertaining in the service of their country - which is not regarded as work. There's been, as some of you know, a long-standing row about payment for diplomatic wives. The Americans are pushing for it and so are several other countries.... And we're not even talking about other obstacles that are less "concrete" - like husbands' objections or the unvoiced but sometimes unmistak-able indirect pressure from employers, certain large corporations in particular.

EG -
The comments that some of the personnel managers we interviewed made about the issue of wives' work were very interesting. Although the majority were aware of the extent of the problem and the reality of the frustration it causes for many

women, there were some who actually denied there was a problem
at all. One man even stated, quite unequivocally, that wives did not
want to work. In view of everything we've been told, we can only
think he had decided to ignore the problem in the hope that it would
go away by itself.

MJ -
Yes, and there was another - I won't tell you the name of the firm
- he was a lovely man.... No, I really mean it - he must have made
a lovely grandfather, very patriarchal, and very crafty! He knew
how important this whole subject is to women: his firm is having
difficulty getting employees to accept transfers because their wives
don't want to give up their jobs. So they've worked out a personnel
policy which is to send young marrieds abroad before the wife's had
a chance to think about her career and thus before she becomes
a problem to the firm. I asked him what happened when these
women eventually went home and tried to take up some sort of
career late in the day, and he looked quite blank - it didn't concern
him any longer.

Anna -
That's nothing new - women have always been pawns in people's
games.

Faith -
Oh yes, I've had a taste of that recently.

MJ -
Hang on, I'm not finished. This man actually said to me - and I'm
quoting him verbatim: "We owe it to the company to select the best,
the 'good couples'. A good home helps a husband to maximize what
he puts into the company." And he ended, without batting an
eyelid: "It's a noble task for a woman."

Anna -
Ha! You see - that's exactly what I mean.

MJ -
Let's not get hot under the collar. They're not all like that,
fortunately. We've talked to some reasonably enlightened personnel managers. Most business firms are now aware of what they call
the "wife problem" (although even that appellation is indicative of
a certain attitude), and they've had to adapt their policies accordingly. They certainly won't openly veto wives working. Many of
them even say they are willing to help with circulating C.V.s and
giving advance information on work permits and so on. They also
say they're now ready to look at the possibility of taking on wives

in their own companies, as long as they are as qualified as any other applicant and are not working directly with their husbands - this still isn't true of many international organizations which have very strict rules about wives and husbands both working within the same organization.

'Things are changing - slowly, to be sure, but changing nevertheless. In fact things have already changed considerably. We're a long way today from the situation of ten years ago.

EG -
We have come across an amazing document. It's the Ladies' Program of a conference held by a large American company in Geneva in 1971. The subject was "How to give your husband the greatest assistance in his job responsibilities". I'll just read you the do's and don'ts:

Do :
1. *Be attractive and gracious*
2. *Be a phone-pal of his secretary*
3. *Be highly adaptable - adjust easily*
4. *Realize he belongs to the company*
5. *Be social*
6. *Be a stabilizer*
7. *Rest and rejuvenate your man*
8. *Be a "sounding board"*
9. *Listen well - talk judiciously*
10. *Aid your husband's public relations*
11. *Handle social obligations*
12. *Practise good conversation*
13. *Put people at ease*
14. *Integrate with local community*
15. *Make constructive friendships*

Don't :
1. *Complain when he works late*
2. *Fuss when a transfer comes up*
3. *Turn up at the office - (emergencies)*
4. *Invite superiors in rank - (wait)*
5. *Get too chummy with wives of associates*
6. *Get tight at a company party*
7. *Wear clothes too blatantly chic*
8. *Make intellectual pretenses*
9. *Talk shop gossip with the girls*
10. *Be disagreeable with company people*
11. *Be too prissy and good*
12. *Engage in controversial activity*

Well, what do you think of that?

Britt -
Wow!

Anna -
I'm not surprised one little bit. And if you think things have changed from those days you should take a look at some of the so-called "wives' seminars" during corporate conventions.

Mary -
I'm speechless. I didn't know people like that existed.

Britt -
You bet they do!

Faith -
They just don't dare to say it openly these days, but that's the message you get nevertheless.

MJ -
Let's calm down and try to think constructively. To sum up, and from the evidence we've got both from employers and - whatever you may think - from many wives as well, employers' policies towards wives *are* getting better. And a lot of women *are* working.

Anna -
Well it is certainly getting easier for European women, at any rate, to get jobs anywhere in the European Community if their country is one of the Twelve.

MJ -
It'll be easier still after 1992, when the Internal Market opens officially. But even now more and more professions can be prac-ticed in different countries within the E.C. and more and more qualifications are being recognized as valid. A British doctor, for instance, can now practice freely in any other E.C. country - and that certainly wasn't the case when I arrived in 1973.

Faith -
But it's very difficult for Americans in Europe to find jobs unless they work for their government or an international corporation or set up their own thing. And even so, they have lots of difficulty with work permits.

MJ -
Yes. You can't get away from that. That's a very big barrier for all

non-E.C. people. But can we talk more generally for a moment? Quite a lot of women who live abroad do work. Not as many as would like to, of course, but quite a few nevertheless. Now, are there jobs that travel better than others? Renate, you're a journalist: this surely is a job that could be considered "portable"?

Renate -
In principle, yes. I simply hope it is true in practice. I'm trying at the moment to build up a list of contacts that I can use wherever I go in the world. But I've had to change the subject I used to cover in Germany. The German public is not interested in what goes on in the theatre in other countries. But, of course, there are other subjects I can cover for German papers. Being a freelance journalist, however, is much harder than being on the staff of a newspaper. You have to consistently produce good work because you're always in the position of selling your stuff and newspapers are under no obligation to take it.

Mary -
I think that teaching is one of the best professions in relation to travelling if there's a big enough international community, or if you're a specialist teacher like a handicapped-children teacher or a remedial teacher.

EG -
There seems to be a particular need for remedial teachers in schools which have a lot of mobile children.

Mary -
Yes, that's absolutely true. Just as there is a special need for school psychologists in international schools, like the European schools here in Brussels, for instance. On the continent also I find that schools often don't have the kind of extra-curricular activities you get in some British schools, for instance. So there's plenty of scope for music, dance or drama teachers.

Joanna -
And don't forget language teaching. That you can take anywhere in the world. Training in teaching your own language is probably the most practical thing you can do if you're going to travel a lot. I know quite a few women who have decided to be trained as teachers of their own language after they have had time to size up what is suitable for their lives.

MJ -
There are, of course, some obvious jobs that are truly international: translating is one of them. Freelance editing also if you are multi-

lingual or if you live in an international city where you can work in your own language. Secretarial work, of course.... and several others. But so much depends on where you live. Living in an international capital or in a place like Geneva is totally different to living in a small provincial town. Brussels is one of the easiest cities to find work in, even for people who do not speak French or Dutch fluently because there are so many international organizations and companies in which you can get away with working in your own language. And above all because there is such a large demand for certain services, such as child-care, counselling and so on.

Mary -
Working with computers is another profession you can take almost anywhere if you're English-speaking because that's the basic language that is used everywhere.

EG -
And there are many more people speaking one or more foreign languages well enough to work in nowadays than there were ten years ago. This is another area that's improved a great deal, and will go on improving. European politicians are increasingly making language-learning a key issue in their training policies.

Anna -
Well, of course. How can you build up Europe if you only speak your own language? It's unthinkable. I'm a convinced European and I think 1992 is going to change a lot of lives. If there was one thing I would suggest to women who are about to go and live abroad and want to find jobs, it's: "Get yourself thoroughly trained in at least a couple of foreign languages."

MJ -
True, but not everyone has a gift for languages or can get good enough tuition to be able to actually work in a foreign language. But there are jobs women can get abroad in which language is not vital, or that don't need an employer on the spot, as it were. I'm thinking specifically of professions that deal with the body: teaching yoga, for instance, or dancing.

'We mustn't forget, also, the possibility of setting up your own business. We've come across a number of women who, either because they couldn't find anything that suited them, or because, like Joanna, they had become aware of a need for a specific product or service in a specific field, have decided to set up business on their own. This ranged from catering - which can be a booming business if you're living in a city like Brussels which is full of international businessmen who like their food - or selling sausages made to an all-American recipe, to setting up a multi-lingual therapy centre, or, more classically, importing goods from your own country.

Joanna -
A Teaching Service is another example - there is one in Brussels. It's a freelance service providing extra tuition for children in their own language. A lot of expatriate children need extra help, for instance when they are going back to their own countries and have been out of the educational system. Some British and American teachers I know work with this organization.

MJ -
There are a lot of good ideas that expatriates have put into practice. We know of several expatriate women's organizations. There's one in Madrid, for instance - it's called Madrid Network - that aims to market its members' skills and try to find them jobs while they are in Spain. There is a similar one in London and at one point W.O.E.* did that in Brussels. One thing Enid and I have felt while working on this book is that there is a place for a Europe-wide organization that could help relocating women find work.

EG -
To go back for a minute to jobs that travel well, there are certain types of work or activities that will most probably benefit from travelling and living in different countries because of the stimulus this gives them, and which are truly "portable". It's what you may call the creative professions: writing, painting, sculpture, photography, crafts of all kinds. Of all the women we have talked to those who least minded moving about from one country to another were those who had made a career out of one of these activities. And there were quite a few of them.

MJ -
Yes, there were. And they were indeed probably the most fulfilled among the women we talked to. But this was because their creative work had actually become a career - i.e. something that they might also have done in their own country, although in many cases it was the necessity of finding a portable career that pointed them in that direction in the first place. What I'm trying to say is that there is a lot of difference between women who would have been artists, writers or whatever at home as well as abroad, and those who take up a creative activity just to fill their time with. Creative work is often solitary work, and a lot of people need the convivial aspect of working with others, especially when they are living abroad where they are already isolated. The real point I'm trying to put across is that if creative work is taken up as a substitute because there is nothing else to do, then it won't be really satisfying in the long run.

*Women's Organisation for Equality

Renate -
I agree with you. This happened to me when I first came to
Brussels. I was frustrated because I was no longer a theatre critic
and I had not yet found the kind of articles to write that could be
sold to German newspapers on a freelance basis, so I decided to fill
my time by writing a novel. But I found that I was missing people,
that time was heavy on my hands, that inspiration just wouldn't
come. I spent most of the time in front of my typewriter waiting for
my husband to come home in the evening.

Britt -
It happened to me also. During one of my many moves I took up
weaving, thinking that I'd become a weaver. But it bored me stiff
after a very short time because I was on my own. I need contact with
people, and continuity in what I do, but with this constant
moving....

Anna -
The need for contact and continuity depend on the kind of person
you are. But so much also depends on the kind of profession you
have. Some professions have a "ladder" structure, that is one in
which you have to progress and climb up steadily and regularly. If
you have had this kind of a career, then moving around is the worst
possible thing.

MJ -
This "ladder" structure reminds me of a talk I heard by a career
counsellor, Elizabeth Dobie, who was lecturing to the British
Diplomatic Service Wives' Association on the problems of women
who want to pursue a career despite interruptions.

'She identified four different patterns in most people's careers, to
which she gave fancy names: the Tree, Snakes and Ladders, the
Snowstorm and the Reflexive.

'The Tree describes careers that progress steadily upwards (like
your "ladder structure", Anna), and that need constant feeding
from the roots - medicine is an example. Snakes and Ladders, she
says, is for careers in which people are forever climbing up then
slipping down.

Britt -
That's me!

MJ -
Then there's the Snowstorm, which she says is more opportunis-
tic - i.e. you take anything that's going, and there's no relation

between the different jobs. It's not a proper career, more a series of disconnected jobs.

Faith -
That's what I had in the States.

MJ -
Then you have the Reflexive, which she visualized like a coil, or a spring mechanism, and which she saw as particularly suitable for women whose careers are interrupted by relocation. If you can visualize a coil - she drew it for us - the flatter sections stand for the periods the women spend abroad, in which they can be training or learning some related skill which can then be used to help the next spring upwards.

EG -
Yes, that's what I've been doing: I took another degree, I am starting training, and hopefully I shall be able to "spring upwards" at the nearest opportunity wherever I go.

Mary -
That's what I've been doing also. Right now I am doing an Open University Course that will boost up my existing degrees and experience.

MJ -
A lot of women we've talked to have used their time abroad to study or get some sort of training. There are a surprising number of university extension courses and international correspondence courses that are being offered in Brussels and other European cities, not to speak of the ubiquitous language proficiency courses.

'One career counsellor, Frances Bastress, who has written a very useful book for relocating spouses - wives or husbands - suggests that the idea of "career" should be taken in a wider sense than its classical definition (i.e. a progressively upward climb in profes-sional life). She thinks it might be taken as describing rather the accumulation of knowledge in one or several fields. In this way, periods of time spent living abroad could be seen as advantageous even if they don't relate directly to a person's profession, but are spent studying or learning a new skill.

Faith -
It sounds similar to what that other lady called the Reflexive pattern.

MJ -
Yes, quite similar.

Joanna -
In a sense certain types of voluntary work - which is sometimes the only kind of work an expatriate can do - can be seen as providing a kind of training that might be useful later on.

EG -
Certainly, and it can give people ideas for their own future, as was the case for you.

Faith -
Yes, but it's also a way to get to know people and to be "recognized". I met a lot of women through doing bits of volunteer work at the American Women's Club. You get to know people and people get to know you, and they say "Oh hello!" when they see you instead of just walking past. Being recognized makes you feel like a person, not another anonymous expatriate.

MJ -
This is a good moment, I think, to broach the subject of voluntary work which is a controversial issue for a lot of expatriate wives.

Anna -
I think it's a controversial subject for women everywhere. For so long, and so frequently, it has been taken for granted that women would do voluntary work and not be paid for it that now, although a lot of women still do it and find fulfillment in it, many others reject it as unsatisfactory because it does not have financial recognition.

Britt -
I think that it is essential to be paid for what you do because it means that someone recognizes your value and is prepared to pay for it. And for me personally it's very important to be actually earning my own money and not feel I'm dependent on my husband for everything.

Anna -
The importance of earning your own money can be resumed in one sentence: it's having control over your own life.

MJ -
All these women who, in the past, have done voluntary work and now have reservations about it - do you think it's a general phenomenon or do expatriate wives feel particularly keenly about it?

Anna -
Both really. More and more women are working and want to work. It's a general social phenomenon, in the West at any rate. But

because it's often the only avenue open to expatriate wives, it becomes in a way symbolic of their situation. It isn't really a choice. You're doing voluntary work because there's nothing else you can do. So after a while you may come to resent it, or, as Joanna said earlier, you may come to feel that you're just "playing" at things.

Joanna -
Yes, this question of choice is, I think, important. Now that I'm working and being paid for it, I would willingly do voluntary work as well. But that would be by choice, not by necessity.

MJ -
Do you think we can recap and pull our ideas together?

'We've looked at how you feel about work in general; we've looked at some of the obstacles that are in the way of expatriate wives finding remunerated work; and we've found that some jobs or careers are more portable than others. It's quite clear that, despite obstacles, there are some women who find satisfying work of some kind, paid or unpaid, wherever they go. What have these women got that other women don't have? It isn't a question of qualifications, I don't think, for some highly qualified women don't find work and some unqualified, or less qualified women do. What is it they have that makes them find what they are looking for?

Anna -
They have to have motivation, to begin with, and that's got to be very strong.... Determination - they mustn't be easily discouraged. And self-confidence.

Mary -
Pushiness. You've got to sell yourself, and you mustn't be afraid to bamboozle people into thinking you've got more experience than you actually have. And, above all, flexibility. If you can't be flexible, forget it! I've met people - women in our position - who, because they were trained in something, say nursing, or accounting, couldn't possibly imagine themselves doing something different, even if it's distantly related to what they trained in. So there they are, still waiting for the ideal job to fall into their lap; and meanwhile they're frustrated, and they moan about it.

'The last time I went for an interview - which was at the school at which I'm now working - the superintendent looked at my C.V. and said: "Marketing assistant? Isn't that a long way from education?" And I said: "Well, look at it this way: in both cases you're selling a line, whether it's in business or in the classroom." And she was broadminded enough to say "Touché", whereas in Ireland, they would most probably have said "That's time lost from education."

Faith -
Are there any special tactics one can develop - I mean concrete things - when one's hunting for a job abroad?

MJ -
This is a question we've asked lots of women who have wanted to work and have found jobs. The consensus seems to be: one, networking - developing contacts and not being afraid to use them; two, thoroughly casing the joint before you get there - from making phone calls, as Mary said, to asking your husband's employers for help, whether in terms of information or in terms of job offers. Three, all the women we talked to stressed that it was was important to get your foot in somehow, even if it wasn't the right job or the right level, because once you're in, you've got more opportunities to move around in that particular firm or that particular area. But also, if you're looking for another job, you're in a different position because you're already employed: you're less of a *demandeur* - which counts psychologically - you have more self-confidence and, of course, you hear much more on the grapevine.

Joanna -
It's quite true that most jobs for expatriates seem to come more via contacts than from advertisements.

EG -
It's worth reading that book Morwenna mentioned, called *The Relocating Spouse's Guide to Employment.** Although it is mostly relevant to American women for specific details, there are general points that are applicable to any women who are subject to geographical mobility. What we thought particularly relevant was the author's emphasis on the need to really understand the situation both in terms of the country you are going to and in terms of your own situation. The author suggests this should be followed by a process of evaluation, looking in the very widest way at what you can do. This may mean using skills you have not used so far in your career, and exploring completely new avenues.

MJ -
Before we close this discussion, I'd like to say that this has been to some extent a one-sided discussion, because all of you, whatever your circumstances - for example Faith's present stage of trying her hand at being a homemaker, or Anna's situation, where she's doing very stimulating work without being paid for it - are women who have worked, want to work and do work. But, as I said at the beginning of this discussion, we must remember that there are

---

* See under BASTRESS in the bibliography

quite a few women who are happy and fulfilled being wives and mothers and enjoying the benefits of living abroad.

EG -
Not to mention the fact that they would have a good point if they criticized us for the implications of our use of the word "work" - as if looking after a house and a family is not work.

MJ -
I know, but we'd have got our tongues all tied up if we'd used the phrase "remunerated work" or "gainful employment" or whatever, instead of "work" throughout this discussion.

'But to go on just a little longer, I do think it is important to remember that many of the difficulties that women abroad experience in looking for, and finding work, are the same for women at home. Take the lack of child-care facilities, for instance, that is often a serious obstacle to women working anywhere. (This in fact can sometimes be easier for them abroad. British or German women coming to Belgium particularly would find it much easier to find good child-care facilities here than in their own countries.)

'Generally, however, I'd say that the difficulties that women experience in their home countries in regard to work are exaggerated when they go abroad, for the reasons we saw earlier. Nevertheless there are many expatriate wives who do work. Quite a few among those we talked to who are employed, told us that the difficulties they had faced had been a challenge to them and had forced them to be creative in a way they might not have had to be at home.'

4

A Prospect of Home

In London
every now and then
I get this craving
for my mother's food
I leave art galleries
in search of plaintains
saltfish/sweet potatoes

I need this link

I need this touch
of home
swinging my bags
like a beacon
against the cold

Grace Nichols
Like a Beacon, from *The Fat Black Woman's Poems*,
London, 1984

Among the women who took part in the discussion that follows were three expatriate wives who were in Brussels on a visit: Rebecca, 55, British, on a visit from Britain; Jennifer, 50, British on a visit from Germany, and Lucy, 37, American, back in Brussels from the United States for a short visit. Also taking part were Yarla, 39, Norwegian, and Sarah, 33, British.

MJ -
Tonight's discussion is, if you all agree, going to concentrate on the notion of "home": how expatriates feel about home when they're abroad; how they feel about going home again; how, when they are actually at home, they view their experience as expatriates; how this has affected them and how they settle back.

'We're very lucky to have here tonight three women who have actually returned to their own countries and can talk about their experience there - they are Rebecca, Lucy and Yarla; and two women - Sarah and Jennifer - who are on the point of going home. I must thank Jennifer particularly because she stopped in Brussels specially to take part in a group discussion. Rebecca and Lucy are also here on a visit and they found time to come and talk to us about their experience. Anyway this is a very special group, I feel, and I'd like to thank you all for coming.

'In addition we've received an interesting letter from Jeanne Daykin*, an ex-expatriate now living in the States, and who heard about our project from her daughter whom we interviewed. We'll be reading parts of her letter at some point in the discussion. Meanwhile, can we have a run-down on each of your histories and experiences? Rebecca, why don't we start with you?

Rebecca -
All right, my name's Rebecca, I'm British, 55, and married to an executive in a large multinational, who is now retired. We have three children, all grown up.

'Robert and I went to live abroad a long time ago - thirty years ago, to be exact - and came back to England two years ago, after my husband retired. Robert started up the Paris office for his organization all those years ago. We'd only recently got married and at first there was just him and myself running the office. I was working fulltime for him, and had a proper salary and all that. Then, when we started a family, I stopped working altogether. By that time the office was bigger.

'From then on I led a very conventional expatriate wife's life. My training had been secretarial, and I really did not miss giving up my

---
*Own name used

job. I wanted to bring up my children and enjoy Paris life unashamedly. I realize now, looking back, that I had a very spoilt and pampered existence - a comfortable lifestyle, a very grand flat, a driver, every kind of help and assistance. Of course it wasn't like that at the beginning, and we did work hard for it.

'I was extremely happy in Paris for the twenty-eight years we spent there. I loved the city, the lifestyle, the friends we made, the cultural aspects. Our children were born and brought up there. Later on, we did the conventional British thing and sent them off to school in England, but they always thought of Paris as home. We all thought of Paris as home. We had a very busy life. I put a lot of time into voluntary activities. But all the time, we knew somewhere that we'd go back to England one day. We were often there on holiday, still had a lot of family there, and knew this was where we'd end up when Robert retired. Which is, of course, what we did.

'I hadn't at all imagined that there would be any problems about going back to Britain. I thought I would just kind of slide back into British life. In the event, we had a real shock.

'It was a very unhappy period for us at the beginning, because of several things. Partly because my husband had retired and this was proving to be quite tough on both of us; partly because we had not realized what life in the English countryside would be like. You know, when you're abroad, you tend to idealize certain aspects of your home country, and Paris is such a "citified" city that the ideal of retiring to the peace of the Cotswolds seemed like a dream. In reality it was terrifically dull and slow-paced. We hadn't realized how much we were going to miss the busy sort of life we'd been living until then. We also had suddenly to face the problem of elderly parents - while we'd been away, other members of the family had had to cope with them. Now it was our turn and we found it very difficult.

'It's only now become clear to me that we've had to start our lives all over again, and with different data. We discovered that neither of us had any role to play in this new environment, and in Paris we'd both been very conscious of what our roles were.

'So, roughly speaking, this is my experience of being back home. Perhaps I'll let other people take over now.

MJ -
You brought up a lot of points there, Rebecca, and I think we should look at them in some detail after other people have given us their histories. Sarah, would you like to tell us about you now?

Sarah -

Everything Rebecca said, reaffirms why I am so keen to go home to Britain now and not live abroad any longer. The difficulty in readjusting to one's own culture and rhythm, the ambiguity of feeling that home may be in a foreign place, while at the same time feeling British and knowing that one would only really want to retire in Britain, the estrangement from reality when one finally goes home - all these are things that I am terrified of. I don't want them to happen to me, and I don't want them to happen to my children.

'I was a diplomatic child myself - my parents were always moving - and later I too joined the Diplomatic Service. So I know what living abroad is all about.

'As a family we had a strong sense of being British, but I could never really say where "home" was. Like Rebecca's children I was at boarding school in England, and I remember envying the other children because they went home to the same place every holiday. And that is what I would like for my children. We were always in different places, we always lived in rented accommodation and had to be careful of the furniture. And we never knew where the Christmas tree was going to go up. I remember feeling that it was terribly important that it should always be in the same corner of the same house every year - but of course this could never be so.

'Despite all this I did join the Foreign Office when I went down from university, and I met my husband, who's a journalist, when we were both working in the U.S. Then he was moved to Brussels. I was extremely reluctant to move. I had just got what I knew was going to be the best job of my life in Washington. However, I gave in, as most women do, relinquished my job, and came to Brussels. I was fortunate in that, within three months, I'd found some interesting work. It helped, of course, that I could speak French fluently and that I'm not a shy and retiring person. Finding work so soon after our arrival probably saved my sanity as well as my marriage. There was an important difference, however, between that new job and what I'd been doing in Washington: quite independently of the work content, I had the feeling that, whereas in Washington I'd been doing a job in my own right, here in Brussels I was in this job because I'd followed my husband to Belgium. Can you understand the difference? I couldn't help feeling I had put myself, or been put by circumstances, in a situation in which I was not doing things in my own right. So I felt that everything I did was very much in his shadow, and his status was very definitely superior to mine, so that added to my slight feeling of being the passive partner, as it were.

'I didn't like Brussels at all at first, and I still don't like it much after three years. Life here is so very artificial, I find. One of the problems with the British is that they tend to stick with the British. It's perhaps understandable in some parts of the world in which the local culture is so very different, but it is also true of Brussels, despite its huge international community. And although we speak three languages, we still tend to mix with British people.

'Another aspect of the artificiality for me is that we have been leading a kind of wild bachelor life here, with champagne flowing, and glamorous week-ends in Paris and Amsterdam. It's got little bearing on reality. And what I now need is to settle into real life. One of the main reasons for this also is that we're starting a family and it's absolutely imperative for me that my children are brought up with a strong sense of their home and country. Although there are great advantages in travelling around, I think it's very important to know where your base is. And when I was living abroad, both as a child and as an adult I would have liked the thought of a particular house in a particular town. I don't want my children ever to feel like that, so, now that I'm pregnant, I can't wait to go home - I now definitely think of Britain as that - which should happen in the next few months.

EG -
Yarla, what about you?

Yarla -
My name is Yarla, I am Norwegian, aged 39, a social worker by training. Like Sarah, I am married to a journalist - only he's Italian - and we have two children, a boy and a girl, aged 8 and 10.

'Like Sarah, I am quite desperate to go home to Oslo, although my reasons are on the whole quite different. I have to say from the start that I've just spent a year in Oslo, with my children, but without my husband, and I have come back to Brussels to see whether it is possible for me to live here again, at least for the length of my husband's posting, which, at the moment is unspecified. But I am finding it extremely difficult.

'One of the reasons for that is that I am obsessed with taking up my career again. As a social worker and a non-Community European (I have always insisted on keeping my Norwegian nationality) it is extremely difficult to find work here, and I am totally fed up with doing voluntary work. What I now want is professional recognition in my own right, and to be paid for the work I do.

'Another reason is that I am also fed up with being a foreigner. I have been one too long. I went to Rome after I was qualified as a social worker, met my husband, Roberto, there, and married him. We moved quite a bit within Italy; first to Milan, then to Turin; then he was posted to the Middle East and eventually to Brussels.

'My children don't know where home is - they were brought up mostly in Italian and French - but I never had any doubts, despite the fact that I have spent nearly fifteen years out of my country. I feel very Norwegian, and despite all the moves, "home" is a certain house - my mother's house - in a certain street in Oslo.

'At the beginning I loved being abroad and I liked the thought of travelling. I felt freer as a foreigner than I had felt at home. I suppose it was not having to conform as I would have done to some extent in Oslo. People make all sorts of excuses for you if you're a foreigner, they'll never treat you as one of their own.

'What I didn't realize until much later is that this kind of freedom is an illusion. You not only feel free because people make excuses for you and treat you differently, but also because you yourself may not understand all the cultural references and the codes of behaviour that surround you. It's a very ambiguous feeling being a foreigner, and I no longer want to live in an ambiguous way. I want to have a steady professional everyday life, an ordinary life if you like, in a country that's familiar in all senses, even if it's far less glamorous than living abroad and even if my standard of living has to come down. In that sense, I feel a little the same way as Sarah.

MJ -
What about your family? Your husband's Italian - how would he feel about living in Norway?

Yarla -
Well, as a journalist, he could ask to be posted there, although it would be a kind of demotion after Brussels where he covers all the E.C. news. But, independently of that, I think he'd find life very difficult there.

'I am afraid at present our marriage is going through a very bad patch. This, of course, though I didn't mention it earlier, is the main reason why I went back to Oslo in the first place. I came back to Brussels because we wanted to have another go at trying to live together. But it isn't easy. If I had a satisfying job here in my own profession, things might become better for us - I'd be less frustrated and less resentful. Or, if we had a better relationship altogether, it might be possible for me to work in Oslo and spend two week-ends a month and all our holidays together. But as it is, it's unthinkable.

EG -
Did you say your children went to Oslo with you for that year?

Yarla -
Yes, I took them along, despite their father's objections. That one year in Oslo was quite an eye-opening experience, both because of being with the children on my own, and because of being in my own country and working.

EG -
You had no difficulty in finding a job as a social worker?

Yarla -
None whatsoever: I got the second job I applied for - within a week of my arrival in Norway - despite the fact that I had not been able to put my training into practice all those years I spent abroad.

MJ -
How did your children adjust to being in Norway?

Yarla -
They were okay because I put them in the French lycée so that there was no break in their schooling; all their schooling, from the time we were in the Middle East onwards, was in French. In Norway they considered themselves as foreigners with one foot in the culture because I am Norwegian. Also when we were in Oslo, we were staying with my mother, so in a sense for them it was a bit like a long holiday.

'I myself think it's a rich experience for children to have the opportunity to live in different cultures. My kids seem quite happy to cultivate their Norwegian field. Perhaps they always wanted to know this part of themselves. So even if we stay in Brussels now, it will not have been a wasted year.

'As for me, being back in Oslo and working was very important. As I said, I feel very Norwegian, and although I'd spent almost fifteen years away (with frequent holidays there, of course) I did not have any difficulty in fitting into life there again. Of course things and people have changed, but it's the same way of thinking, the same references. It felt so... how shall I say?... easy.

'I was leading a rather proletarian life in Oslo during that year, taking the tram like everybody else at seven in the morning, working all day, then doing things with the children. I didn't have time to have much of a social life, but I felt happy because the life I had I had made for myself.

'In Brussels our life had been very luxurious. We went to the theatre and to the cinema whenever we liked; there was never any problem with babysitters, househelp or anything like that. But it never felt quite real - not so much because of the higher standard of living, but because there wasn't any real quality of life to go with it. I need a life that feels real to me, and I came to realize in the end that being abroad would never bring me that. Reality for me is connected to self-realization, to making bonds that are based on shared values and references, and so on.

MJ -
So do you think you will return to Oslo?

Yarla -
I still don't know. It depends on whether things work out between my husband and myself and on whether I am able to find a suitable job here in Brussels. At the moment things are very much up in the air and it is a difficult period for all of us.

MJ -
Now, Jennifer, you're on the point of going home, aren't you, after a long time spent going round airforce bases everywhere. Can you tell us a bit about yourself?

Jennifer -
Yes, all right. I'm British, just turned fifty and my husband's a chaplain in the R.A.F. We have three children. We're going home to Britain - hopefully for good - in two weeks' time. Bill's leaving the service, and that's not an easy thing to do, I can tell you.

MJ -
What do you mean?

Jennifer -
Well, when you sign on for the Services, you really do sign your life away. They can actually stop you going until you're fifty and even later it isn't that easy. You're not free, you know. The Queen owns you 24 hours a day - and you will work 24 hours a day if she tells you to work 24 hours a day - and you go where she tells you to go. You don't have any choice in the matter.

Sarah -
So how did you come to leave the Service?

Jennifer -

Well, I downed tools, I suppose. We'd just been on a posting to Germany, one of many postings - too many. In 25 years of married life I've lived in Britain for less than six, and I've lived in 18 different houses. I felt I'd had it with Service life. It's too alienating for a wife.

'So we'd been in Germany for two and a half years and we knew we'd be moving again soon. We'd been studying the list of possible postings - that's what people in the Services do all the time, you know - and Bill had asked to go to one particular place so that we could be nearer to our children, who are at university and school in Britain. Then one day he came in and said, "I don't know how to tell you...." And of course his news was that the posting was somewhere that to me was unthinkable. So I said, "Well, I'm just not going, and that is it."

'As it happened the week before Bill had seen an interesting ad in *The Church Times* for a job in Britain. So when we knew about the posting, he applied without telling anybody. When he was told he was being short-listed, however, he had to come clean about it. And what a fuss they made about it! It was a terrible crime to apply for another job, out of the Services, a terrible disloyalty. This was TROUBLE in capital letters. Bill was summoned to headquarters to be rebuked. So he told them I had put my foot down, and since they don't like domestic scandals and he was over fifty anyway, they let him go.

'So here we are, we shall be back in Britain in two weeks' time, and I just can't wait to be near the children, to have a house of my own, to be free, finally, of this awful feeling of being owned by the State.

EG -

Lucy, I remember that when you came to a group discussion here about two years ago, you also were on the point of going home for good, and you couldn't wait to get there. How do you feel now that you're living in the United States once again?

Lucy -

Ah, that's not a simple thing to explain. But first I guess I must introduce myself.

'My name's Lucy, I'm an American, 37 years old this month. I 'm married to an accountant, and we have no children. Like Yarla I'm a social worker by training and vocation. We've lived in New York all our lives until we came to Brussels for a relatively short stay - three years - and now we've been back in the States for one year.

'We came to Brussels on a three-year contract that we knew was non-renewable from the start - otherwise I doubt I would have said yes to following Pete abroad. It was the first time either of us had lived abroad. We'd come to Europe for holidays, but of course that's always quite different, and I don't really think I had any illusions about that.

'What I had illusions about was all the things this extended sabbatical was going to allow me to do. I hadn't reckoned, however, with the sort of formidable inner culture shock you get when you find yourself sitting at home all day in a totally alien place, waiting for your husband to come home, when formerly you were a self-assured, financially independent career woman. This kind of sapped me. In fact I had a sort of depression or nervous breakdown, although I didn't recognize it as such until much later. It was quite early on in our move that I started feeling uneasy. I first noticed it in little things, like feeling that my clothes didn't look right, that the things in the closet all looked terrible. Then I started putting on weight and found it more and more difficult to look at myself in the mirror, but I still didn't connect it to what I was feeling inside. I criticized everything and everybody, and my husband would say when I kept complaining, "Why are you always trying to change things and people?" It felt as if everything was wrong, and I couldn't see that what was wrong was me.

'Anyway it took about a year to sort myself out, and then it became imperative that I should forget the idea of an extended leisure-filled sabbatical and start doing something that stimulated me and that might be useful to me in the future. So I did a university extension course at one of the American universities in Brussels and finished it just as Pete's contract came to an end. So I was very happy to go home again - you're quite right, when I came to that group discussion at that point, I just couldn't wait to be back in New York and take up the threads of my life again, to get back into the mainstream, which to me, means my work. (Also, I have to admit, the weather here in Brussels had really got me down and I was more than ready for a change of climate.)

'However things were not as easy as I thought they would be. No sooner had I returned to the States than I had to have major, though routine, surgery, which set me back a few months and I've spent the last six months doing a very broad job search using the second masters degree I worked on in Belgium. As you may know, social services are in a mess with the economic situation in the U.S. and the direction the government has been taking. No one seriously expects any improvement in the foreseeable future. Seeing Europe, the pride and dignity people generally have, which are partly the result of a social welfare-oriented system, and facing the bleak outlook for change in the U.S. made me realize that I had to do some real soul-searching about what I can do professionally.

MJ -
Are you thinking of leaving social work?

Lucy -
This is still unclear. I am applying for administrative and planning positions (and this means that I'll probably have to develop some new and stimulating outside interest, like painting, which I enjoy, to keep my sanity). So, from what I see now, the experience of living in Europe has become very much interwoven with who and what I am and want to be. This is not to say I am always so positive. The past year in the States and the past four years generally have at times been very difficult and I have questioned what I've done and whether it was right.

Sarah -
What does your husband feel about all this?

Lucy -
Ah, this is a sensitive subject. I had felt, when we came to Brussels, that I had made the choice to follow him fully consciously. But while here, after thinking, and reading, and finding myself in the unfamiliar role of wife/housewife rather than autonomous, working wife, talking to other women who regularly follow their husbands from country to country, I began to see how in many ways I had accommodated, often uncomfortably, to my husband's desires and goals for fourteen years.

'Living abroad did not cause problems that had not existed before, but the situation - particularly the fact that I wasn't working - did exacerbate existing difficulties. It also rather severely strained my previous concept of myself as a fully functioning, capable person, which probably placed even more stress on the situation.

'I am not living with my husband at present, having told him before we left Belgium that my ability to get a meaningful job would determine whether I would stay with him. Since he is likely to get transferred again, within the States, I'm looking for jobs in a number of areas and states, including near where he is or is likely to be transferred, but I view the future with a fairly wary eye, for I do question, after the experience I had in Belgium, whether any relationship could fill the strong need I have to do as much with myself as I can, and unfortunately I have found that neither I nor this need pack and travel well.

MJ -
Perhaps at this stage we should recap. Each of you has raised a number of points that are important and echo what other women have told us. But what I also find interesting in this particular group discussion is that we obviously have here very different attitudes to both the prospect and the reality of "home". Some of these attitudes are themselves ambivalent, and this is not surprising: we found out during our research that expatriates often seem ambivalent and sometimes confused about the idea of home.

'So here we have Rebecca, who thought of Paris as home, but knew she would one day retire in Britain, and is shocked at how difficult it can be sometimes to be back in one's own culture. We have Lucy, whose stay abroad has enabled her to step back and take a long look at her own needs as well as the state of her profession in her country. We have Yarla, who feels that living abroad, being a foreigner is somehow evading "real life", and who is torn between the desire to patch up her marriage and the desire to go back to "real life" in her country. Then we have Jennifer and Sarah who are not at all ambiguous about their wish to go and settle in Britain for good and live a steady life in a familiar place.

'I'd like to pick up one or two of the more important themes that have emerged from what you have said and discuss them a bit further. May I suggest that we start, for instance, with the idea that life abroad feels unreal to a lot of women.

Lucy -
Yes, I was interested to hear Yarla saying, a while back, that even after fifteen or so years abroad, she still feels that living in a foreign country is unreal. I'd always assumed that this unreality (which I also felt when I was living in Brussels) was due to the fact that we were literally taking three years out of the normal run of our lives. Do you think this is always so, or is it mostly women who are moving frequently, or just once like me, who feel that?

EG -
It's actually a very difficult thing to nail down. We've met women who are uprooted by their husbands' employers every three, four or five years, and who seem to have integrated mobility as a way of life - so that it has become part of their "real" life. We've met other women, who even after ten years or more in the same place, still feel there is something unreal about their life abroad. So much depends on character and adaptability, and so much on whether a woman finds a fulfilling occupation, good friendships and so on.

'Part of the unreality, at least at the beginning of a move, whatever its length is going to be, is that when you first move to a foreign country, nobody knows who you are, or what you are, so there is a certain loss of identity. Part of it also may be due to this "inner culture shock" Lucy was talking about, when a woman who had been working and independent in her own country suddenly finds herself in a totally different role - that of a housebound wife/mother. And part of it - which many women feel even if they've been living in one place for many years - may be due to the fact that foreigners rarely get very involved with what goes on in their host country, at a political or social level. At the same time they have lost the possibility of being really involved at grass-roots level in what goes on in their own country. So they're floating between two worlds, they're always on the outside looking in.

MJ -
Also for a lot of people moving abroad brings a change in lifestyle and standard of living, which makes the gap between their life at home and their life abroad even bigger, thus emphasizing their sense of unreality.

Yarla -
I think that for me, and for a lot of women of my generation, reality and day-to-day life are entirely defined in terms of career and work, and if this is what you expect of life and you don't get it it automatically puts you in a situation of unreality.

Jennifer -
I'm a different generation from you. Women of my generation didn't really expect to be employed after having children, and I think one of my problems is that I never really got involved in a career. Of course I might have had to abandon it after Bill joined the R.A.F., but I might nevertheless have developed a competence that might have been put to some use.

'Service life is terribly unreal, you know, however many years you serve. When we first joined, they were twenty years out of date with the rest of the world. Now they're only ten years out of date. It is also totally out of touch with the immediate world around it. For a long time, for instance, nobody lived off camp. We were among the first to move out. A Service community is a self-contained bubble: it has schools, shops, hospitals, men's clubs, wives' clubs, everything. You need never go outside. It's like living in a huge World War Three shelter.

'You often even can avoid mixing with other Services within the same area. In Gibraltar, for instance, we hardly mixed with anybody who wasn't in the Airforce, because we were north of the runway, and it's very difficult to get over it - it's a hassle, they shut down the barriers.

'Also any Service creates its own hierarchies which rub off onto wives and children. You have an airmen's wives' club, for instance, that is for airmen's wives and up to warrant officers' wives only. Officers' wives did not go to it - they wouldn't have been welcome. You wouldn't have gone to an airmen's wives' club without being invited anymore than you'd go into someone else's house without being invited.

'In Gibraltar we moved into the Airforce officers' "patch", where we had a beach, which was an enormous perk. We didn't mix and the other Services felt the Airforce was very uppity and exclusive. We were the only ones to have a beach. Everyone else was clinging to the sides of the cliff.

'You're so cut off from real life that in a sense you get brainwashed. Your mind turns to blubber because there is no intellectual stimulation whatsoever. This is why so many Services wives have the reputation (deservedly, I'm sure) of being alcoholics.

MJ -
Yes, we read reports about that. The figures were quite staggering.

Jennifer -
I'm not surprised. I must say the general atmosphere seems to be getting a little better now in the Airforce. For one thing they take in graduates these days and this means that their wives are often more highly qualified too. We had a curate, for instance, in one of our postings, whose wife was a sociologist. She was quite bloody actually, kept herself to herself, walking about everywhere in a black anorak, refusing to look the part. She was probably preserving herself by doing it. I thought at the time she was being a bit silly, but I had been brainwashed by how people are expected to behave and look in the Services. We're very much in a mould, conservative, don't say what we actually mean. We have a patter. After all we have to live with one another and at very close quarters. The only consolation is that people move on.

Sarah -
How dismal!

Jennifer -
Oh, dismal it was. It was very alienating. I felt extremely envious of my friends at home who were working. There was one friend in particular, whom I'd first met in Gibraltar. Her husband had gone

to an Airforce base back home and she'd got a job in the post office in the mornings. I was terribly envious of her: to me this was the acme of desirability! I think she earned about two pounds an hour, and I felt I couldn't even do this.

'So you see, life always felt very unreal and alien to me, even though we were not living abroad in the midst of an alien community. We were, to all intents and purposes, living in a narrow sort of Britain in foreign territories. And certainly, in our case, my feeling of unreality did not come from a grander lifestyle or standard of living.

'Obviously you do have more money, but living abroad may be very expensive because you have to do the British thing and send your children to boarding schools at home. The Services do pay school fees, but you want to visit them often, and expenses pile up.

'You live in houses according to your rank, not to the size of your family. So if you're an Air-Marshal, you may have six to eight bedrooms even though you might be childless, whereas if you're a flight-lieutenant, you'll have a two-and-a half-bedroom house even if you have ten children. Bill was entitled to four bedrooms, but on one of our postings, when the children were still living with us, we found that all the money had been spent on the bloody runways, so we only had two and a half bedrooms. Yet in the same place you have people a little higher up in the hierarchy, who have four bedrooms and no children.

'I became crosser and crosser with each move, so when this last posting came up, I found I couldn't live this unreal life any longer.

Rebecca -
I think I'm alone amongst all of you to feel that life abroad was not unreal. On the contrary, I very much felt it was my life. I brought up my children abroad and that's where I felt our home was. In fact what was unreal was coming back to England. Living in Gloucestershire after Paris was an unimaginable shock. I did find a job eventually, not a high-powered one, just secretarial work, but that was my salvation. So much depends, when you go back to your own country, on whether you have a groove to slide into. If you had a career before you left or some job you can go back into, then it's all right. But if you haven't, then you're just a middle-aged woman who has lived abroad.

MJ -
The problem is that even if you did have a job or a career before you went to live abroad, it isn't quite as easy as all that to slide back into the groove as you say. It's a constant rat race on the employment

market, and if you lose your place in the race, you may not find it again. Things change when you've been away. You're in the same position after even a shortish stay abroad as you are at home when you've taken a few years off work to bring up your children, and you suddenly want to get back into the job market. It can be very difficult, and meanwhile you have lost some self-confidence.

EG -
I'd like to go back to Rebecca for a minute. How much of this kind of counter-culture shock do you think was due to the fact that, with your husband's retirement, your circumstances had changed?

Rebecca -
Oh, a lot of it, I'm sure. Not only was there a big difference in our standard of living because we were living on his pension, with no perks and so on, but also I think that retirement affected his self-image, the image other people had of him, and generally the roles we had made for ourselves in Paris. It was as, I think, Lucy called it an "inner culture-shock" as much as an environment culture shock, because a lot of it was due to the place we were living in. Things got much better after we decided to move to a flat in London, but we could only do this after both my parents had died.

'But, to get back to the unreality of life - which I can truly say I never felt while I was living in Paris - I can understand what you mean by it. Curiously, when I go back to Paris now on a visit and see my old friends there, it seems rather bizarre, all this St George's Society business and other such expatriate activities. After a period in England it feels like the Sixties and Seventies - a lot of people filling their lives with voluntary activities because they haven't been able or willing to find something really useful to do.

Lucy -
After being in England a couple of years you cannot help looking at Paris with a different perception. The reverse happened to me after a couple of years in Belgium. I started to look at the United States with a different perception which was of course coloured by the stereotypes that Europeans have of the U.S. - the big cars, the litter, fast foods, crime rate, racism and so on. Perhaps because of my sociological background, and perhaps also because I haven't been back all that long, this perception has remained in me. It's made me more sensitive to all these things.

MJ -
I think I mentioned at the beginning of the discussion that we've had a letter from Jeanne Daykin, who writes from Peoria, Illinois, and who has done a lot of work on counter or reverse culture shock

as it is called, which is the difficulty in adjusting to being back in one's own country that quite a few expatriates seem to experience.

'Jeanne lived in Brussels for fifteen years with her husband and three daughters - one of whom is now once more living in Brussels, this time with her British husband, who is a journalist. Jeanne and her family were very happy in Europe, and even bought and restored an old farmhouse in the Dordogne. As she says, culture shock never materialized for her, although her eldest daughter had some problems adjusting to the disruption in her school and social life.

'Eventually Jeanne's husband was moved back to the States, and although they have a lovely house and one of their daughters lives half an hour away with her own family, and they are surrounded by other relatives and a few good friends, Jeanne has found it difficult to adjust to living in the United States after so many years in Europe. She writes:

"...I am not content. For the first time in my life I know what it is to be depressed. My marriage has suffered as well and I have consulted a therapist in the hope I can come out of my depression. I miss the excitement and frustrations of life in a foreign country. I am a victim of reverse culture shock. I've found out I am not alone.

"Many women I have talked to have enjoyed the time they spent abroad, and they are equally happy to be back. Others are not. They feel that the time they spent abroad was wasted. The things they learned there are of no value to them now. They, and more often their children, feel alienated in their own country. Some feel that life abroad led to serious problems in their lives. Perhaps the statistics concerning divorce, alcohol and drug abuse, even the rare suicide, attest to that. Of course these problems are endemic in our society today, but it is certainly plausible that the overseas experience might be a contributing factor in our lives."

'As was the case with ourselves, her own experience and her discussions with other women spurred her to start a survey about the phenomenon of reverse culture shock and she had a lot of response from women who had moved back to the United States after one or several moves abroad.

'In a short article called "Displaced Americans Abroad and Back", she writes that although a poll by Korn-Ferry recruiters, reported in *The Wall Street Journal,* found that more than half the managers questioned described "re-entry problems", very little consideration had been given to the same phenomenon among their families.

'Another thing she talks about is the attitude of the people "back home" to returning expatriates, saying that the advice given by an organization called F.A.W.C.O. (Federation of American Women's Clubs) following a study they made of reverse culture shock was "Don't talk about your overseas experience unless specifically asked."

Lucy -
Oh, yes, I know all about that. People back home just don't want to know about it. It obviously bothers them, they even get hostile about it. It's as if you're brandishing your difference and one-upmanship in their face. We Americans are so insecure!

MJ -
She was particularly concerned about the effect on children. In that same article she sent us, she writes: *"Some younger children try to hide the fact from their teachers and class-mates because they resent being considered odd or different. They put up with that when they lived in a foreign country and find it unfair and confusing when it reoccurs here at home. Our youngest daughter was seven when we moved abroad and had only visited the States for occasional brief holidays before she returned for college. At school only her closest friends were aware that she had ever lived in a foreign country. Even now she'll send me a warning glance if I speak about that time to anyone who doesn't already know. She's learned that even casual comments about ordinary happenings in her everyday life abroad might create feelings of envy and even enmity in potential friends.*

"Our children's needs to conceal a time in their lives that was so remarkable must surely have an adverse effect on them psychologically. It's not surprising when they suffer from Reverse Culture Shock and a feeling of alienation long after their return."

Sarah -
I concur with that having been a Foreign Office child at boarding school in England. I always felt the odd one out and took great pains to hide the extent of my foreign experiences. This is why I want to make sure that my children do not experience the same feelings. To me the thought of going home is very much linked with the idea of starting a new life and giving my children the stability I lacked.

MJ -
Yes, it's a very different experience because you are young and you have both your professional and family life ahead of you. But a lot

of people we've interviewed or discussed the subject with, are
ambivalent about going home, not only because they don't quite
know how they, and the people around them, are going to react, but
because for most of them, going home means retirement - a very
big step in someone's life. So unconsciously they connect the idea
of going home with a kind of early death.

Rebecca -
I agree with you here. I'm sure that this is what lay at the bottc ͗ɹ
of our feelings of depression when we first moved back to England.
More than the drop in standard of living and the dull country
environment (which was itself a kind of burial - we did feel "buried"
in the middle of the countryside -) it was the fact that being back
home meant that the active part of our life was finished. It felt like
the end of the journey.

MJ -
So, to sum up, what do you think the prospect of home means to
expatriates?

Jennifer -
I think it represents everything that being abroad is not: family,
stability, warmth, security, normality. I remember my daughter
saying to me once that she wished she could come home from
school in the afternoons and find me baking apple pie in a large
English kitchen. You see she was at boarding school most of her
life and this kind of scene was something she'd never known.

Lucy -
This is the kind of image someone thinks of when they're homesick
- like Sarah's Christmas tree. But the trouble is that when you've
been away for a time these images get fixed and stop relating to
reality. They become fantasy, a myth, a symbol of everything you
are homesick for. Just as when one grows up - and I mean anyone,
not just expatriates - one idealizes certain images of childhood,
certain places. Call it nostalgia, fantasy, wishful thinking, whatever, but it's got no bearing on reality. What's real is that things
change, people change, nothing ever remains the same, and we
must all learn to accept that.

'I remember when we graduated from college, our principal made
a speech in which he said that when we went home we shouldn't
be surprised or shocked to find that things were very different from
what we remembered and expected, because in the years we'd been
away (many of us came from a long way away and hadn't been home
in four years) not only would things at home have changed - after
all life doesn't stand still - but we, too, had changed, and all our

perceptions had changed.

EG -
I think your principal was absolutely right, and that what he said applies very well to a lot of expatriates.

'One of the differences between the shock of going to live abroad and the shock of going to live at home again is that perhaps when you first go to live in a foreign country, you're going out into the blue into something that's basically open-ended (even if the move is a short-lived one), and may reserve a lot of surprises and stimulation, even if it isn't obvious at first. Whereas when you go home, you think you're returning to something that is safe and known and familiar.

'And because so many people tend to think of their time abroad as a chunk taken out of the normal course of their lives, they believe that life at home will to a great extent have stood still, that when they go back they can just pick up where they left off. Even when they've been back on holidays, and are aware, somewhere, that things have changed, when they go back home to live, they are amazed that things cost so much more, that places have changed, that relationships are no longer the same, and above all, that the people they love have got older. It's very painful, and it can cause quite a shock because suddenly you realize that you, too, have changed, and that you, too, have got older.

'And perhaps it isn't just realizing that you have changed and got older. I think that you are suddenly made more aware of time in a brutal way. In a sense, for some people, going home may be an intimation of mortality.'

IV

MOVING FIGURES IN A MOVING LANDSCAPE

1

The New Nomads

Travel they say improves the mind,
An irritating platitude
Which frankly, entre nous
Is very far from true.....

Refrain: Why do the wrong people travel, travel, travel,
When the right people stay back home?

Noël Coward,
Why Do the Wrong People Travel ?
from *Collected Lyrics*, London, 1965

In Anita Brookner's *Hôtel du Lac* [1] there is a character called Monica who is a British expatriate, a 'languid and luxurious woman', with a greedy little dog and a husband who is 'something important in Brussels'. She is staying at a Swiss lakeside hotel, out of season, for her health. Bored, critical, limp, broody, cynical, depressed, shrewd and observant, she 'eats far too many cakes for one so thin' and wears habitual lines of discontent on her beautiful face. She is an infuriating, sad, doomed, yet curiously sympathetic character, despised by her husband and full of sluggish self-loathing. She, a writer's image of a modern expatriate wife, is the memsahib's grandaughter.

The memsahib! What images this word evokes. Of all the types of people that the great colonial empires - the French, the Spanish, the Portuguese, above all the British - produced, none was more vivid, more controversial, more misunderstood than their women, or rather, their wives.

Like all popular images, the one that grew around the figure of the memsahib oversimplifies and caricatures. If gossip and intrigue were the hallmarks of colonial communities everywhere, women were always taken to be their main perpetrators and purveyors. Given this image, it is not surprising that in British India, for instance, the women's annexe to men's clubs was known as 'the hen-house' or, more graphically, 'the snake-pit'.

And like all images, this does not take into account the many women who refused to fit into the conventional mould, who would have died of boredom or frustration had they not found other pursuits and interests than those normally available to their class and sex, and who, in moments of political unrest or rebellion, or when natural disasters struck, showed that they, too, like some of their men, were capable of heroic behaviour and selflessness.

Most of the writers whose work is largely associated with colonial life - among them Kipling, Somerset Maugham, Conrad, John Masters and Paul Scott - did little to offset or correct the derogatory image of the memsahib, although they sensed at times that behind the idleness, the gossip and the intrigue lay unhappiness, bitterness and isolation.

So it was left to historians to view the situation of colonial women with greater perspective and insight: 'The notorious absurdities of the memsahibs, satirized for so long by male writers', writes Jan Morris in her triptych on the British Empire, 'were generally only the frustrated expressions of unhappiness, fear, homesickness and waste - for surrounded as she generally was by servants, denied any real responsibility, the woman of the Empire often felt herself to be no more than an ornamental, and progressively more un-ornamental, supernumary. Nobody wanted her to be too clever, still less politically concerned. Any attempt to break from the herd would damage her husband's career.... Male values were supreme almost everywhere in the British Empire, and even the family role, even motherhood itself, was forlornly disrupted by constant partings.' [2]

What is acceptable and understandable in this description of a nineteenth-century colonial wife becomes disturbing when one realizes that much of it echoes statements made by modern expatriate wives about themselves.

In both cases, the woman's role has been to follow her husband, with all that this may entail; in both, her life is marked by partings, transience and alienness; in both the woman draws a vicarious status and reputation; in both she leads a life of relative ease - though here again, in both cases, the myth often exaggerates the reality of material benefits; in both the woman is frequently isolated within an expatriate community, with its emphasis on maintaining traditions and rituals, its enforced closeness and the subsequent lack of integration with the surroundings; in both, potentials for individual growth are often stunted or made difficult by the pressures of the situation.

It would, however, be short-sighted and misleading to assume that the modern expatriate woman is the memsahib's grandaughter and only the memsahib's grandaughter. For, if the memsahib was a product of her age, so too is the modern expatriate wife - a child of the latter half of the twentieth century - whose image of herself and what she expects of life, despite pressures and circumstances that sometimes conspire to keep her within a prescribed role, have radically changed.

****

Who, then, are these modern women who follow their husbands across frontiers and oceans, from country to country and continent to continent, leaving behind relatives and friends, homes and careers, the familiar, the safe, the loved, for the insecurity and strangeness of life in a foreign land or the repeated disruptions of a nomadic experience? Who and what are they, and why do they do it?

The sample used to prepare this book covers women from all major areas of expatriate life, from the most protected and secluded, such as the armed forces, to the most isolated in terms of support systems, such as independent businesses.

These women's husbands work for large companies, international organizations, foreign services, the armed forces; they are teachers, journalists or representatives of religious bodies. Many are experts on secondment from their government or institution to foreign governments or international organizations, or work as consultants to national or international companies.

The nature of these men's professions has entailed one or several periods of working and living abroad. For many this was not a way of life they had envisaged when they first began their career but something that cropped up as it developed. Others, like diplomats or members of the armed forces, knew that the profession they had chosen imposed an extensive experience of mobility.

The women who took part in our study came from twenty-eight different countries and their ages ranged from 24 to 58. Their economic and educational background places the majority in the middle class.

The large majority of these women have high educational and professional qualifications. 76% of them have university degrees - some with post-graduate qualifications; many others have received vocational training of some kind. Their professions include teaching (from primary to university level), social and probation work, nursing, medecine, psychology, psychoanalysis, therapy of various kinds, biology, anthropology, pharmacy, computer work, research, business and real estate administration, fashion, banking, accountancy, secretarial work, journalism, writing, music, dancing, the civil and diplomatic services, photography, archeology, architecture, arts and crafts.

16% of the 300 women had never been employed; prior to going abroad, 26% had interrupted their careers temporarily or left their jobs when they had children. Of the 58% who were employed when their husbands' profession took them abroad, the majority felt that the move had been disruptive to their own career.

Given these women's qualifications and the fact that over half of them previously held jobs or careers that they felt to be important to them, it seemed surprising that so many had decided to follow their husbands abroad.

To the question of whether they had been in total agreement with their husbands' decision to go and work in a foreign country, 75% of the questionnaire respondents answered yes, 15% answered no, and the rest gave mitigated, non-committal answers. It was in the course of interviews and group discussions, however, that the ambiguous nature of many situations was revealed.

'What could I do?' said Barbara, an American biologist, married to an engineer and now living in Rome. 'The post abroad was a big promotion for my husband, a turning-point in his career, and the job content itself was exciting. I did not feel entitled to say "Don't take it, *my* career comes first." Nor could I refuse to follow him because I felt that living so far apart might well end up breaking the marriage. So you see, I didn't really have any choice. Or rather my choice was to either follow him to Rome or risk losing him. So I made up my mind, but it did not feel like a real choice.'

The majority of the women who had been employed in their own countries, highly qualified though they were, were nevertheless in a financial position that was unequal to their husbands', and felt that this did not give them enough bargaining power to oppose a move.

Lorna, an Australian expatriate, identified a different and often unvoiced or unacknowledged level of pressure which makes some working women give priority to their husband's career when they are faced with the decision of moving abroad. Lorna had been highly successful in her career as a real-estate administrator and, in her last job, which she left when her husband was transferred to Europe, she had thirteen people working under her. 'We spent many hours talking about whether Ian should not follow me for a change, and we always came back to the fact that, of the two, he is the bigger wage-earner. 'But', she went on, 'there is something else as well: do you not think that, in a way, job security and working in general are far more important for a man than for a woman? What I mean is that deep down I feel the man is not going to be able to cope if he has not got a job. Yes, I can take it, but can he? And I can live with my unhappiness, but can he?'

Beyond the basic professional reason for which their husbands were sent abroad, women acknowledged other reasons, some concrete, some not, that had attracted them. For the majority, it was the lure of a higher salary and standard of living, coupled with a feeling of adventure, challenge and curiosity at seeing other cultures at close quarters. Many also acknowledged that it was an escape - from routine, relatives, dilemmas, problems - a chance to get off the treadmill, a breathing space.

Other women said they had been motivated by ideological or humanitarian reasons. Many of these had husbands who worked for international organizations such as the European Community, the World Health Organization, U.N.I.C.E.F., and so on, and were strongly supportive of the nature of their spouses' work. Others were married to clergymen or missionary teachers. Here too, their questionnaires revealed great support for their husbands' professions. One of these women wrote: 'My situation is probably a little different from most of the women who will be surveyed, in that coming here was totally a joint decision by my husband and myself, and I'm very involved in the work with him. Another factor that influences my attitude on being here and my perspective on the country and people is that I have a personal relationship with God, so I know that anywhere I'm serving Him, He will give me the strength and ability to adjust to that culture and function adequately. We saw things work out in such incredible ways to give us the opportunity to come here that we feel the Lord has a purpose for us being here.'

Despite these motivations, few women expressed definite goals for themselves. Most concentrated, when thinking about the advantages of going abroad, on the opportunities to travel, to meet new people and get to know new cultures and environments. Those who mentioned any advantages gained for their own work were few and far between. An archaeologist, for instance, hoped to profit by joining in excavations: an anthropologist living in southern Spain was glad of the opportunity to do field work there. Some saw the period abroad as a chance to study, write a thesis, or a book, take a doctorate; others wanted to develop talents they had not had time to develop at home. Only a very small number, however, had seriously researched the possibility of working before going abroad.

****

The society that has produced the modern expatriate is itself a society on the move.

Its transformation, from an agricultural to a mechanized society, then from a mechanized to a super-industrialized society, and the ever-galloping progress of technology, has established an internationalization of resources, techniques and products. The effect of this, in terms of work force, has been similar to that of the opening up of the great colonial empires. But while geographical mobility between countries still concerns a relatively small number of people, the population within each country is itself far from sedentary. Indeed, geographical mobility in general has become such a vital part of modern life that one might be tempted to paraphrase William H. Whyte's famous remark about American society, and state that 'the man who leaves home is not the exception in Western society, but the key to it'.[3]

The increasing institutionalization of mobility is reflected in language. The word 'relocation' and its derivatives, for instance, have passed into officialese. And, while the people who are directly affected are described as 'modern nomads' or 'corporate gipsies' and so on, their wives or husbands are given the less romantic, if graphic, appellation of 'trailing spouses'. Familiarity breeds jokes, the most famous being that I.B.M., to those who work for that company, stands for 'I've Been Moved'.

Experience has shown that mobility is far from neutral in its effect on people. Since the end of World War II, Western society, with American society in the lead, has been increasingly described as a 'throwaway society'. The sense of impermanence that already pervades a world in which today's technological breakthroughs will be obsolete by next Christmas, is reinforced by the fact that more and more people are moving, and that they are moving more and more frequently. Concepts and institutions which, in the past stood for stability - the family, long-standing relationships, a sense of place - have undergone a drastic change: the traditional extended family has become increasingly nuclearized and its former values have been eroded. Constant partings and distance have undermined the secure-making strength of close relationships. As for the sense of place, it has by now acquired a positively mythical value. Concepts hitherto taken for granted - such as roots, or distance - have to be reassessed in the light of these changes.

'Never in history', wrote Alvin Toffler in 1970, 'has distance meant less. Never have man's relationships with place been more numerous, fragile and temporary. Throughout the advanced technological societies, commuting, travelling and regularly relocating one's family have become second nature. We are breeding a new race of nomads.'[4]

****

Set against a background of increasing mobility within countries, the women who follow their husbands abroad no longer seem such a rare breed and, as the numbers of organizations operating internationally grow, it is obvious not only that their number will increase, but also that their situation will be more publicized.

The remarkable proliferation of such organizations is a twentieth-century phenomenon but one which may, historically, be traced back to the Industrial Revolution, to the new technologies and industries of the nineteenth century and their repercussions on political and social structures.

It is in the nineteenth century that the beginnings of international cooperation may be found, in such bodies as the international trade unions or in the first 'Great Power' conferences, as they were called. The creation of the League of Nations after the First World War and, later, the birth of the big international organizations, were the logical outcome of that international cooperation. The goals of the United Nations - which seek to maintain international peace and security, the development of friendly relations among nations, and the achievement of international cooperation - are a development of nineteenth-century aspirations.

These are also some of the goals which lie behind the creation of the European Community, hard though it may be to distinguish them in the dry terms of the Treaty of Rome - the founding charter of the European Economic Community.

These institutions depend for their success on a deeply-held belief: namely that, despite historic rivalries between nations, people might be found who would work, not just for their own country, but for the interests of groups of countries. This is the basis on which the secretariats of the different international institutions function.

Ideas such as these led to the remarkable growth of international organizations which followed the two World Wars, more particularly the Second. Indeed, since 1943, their number has grown from ten to 337. The largest of these, the United Nations, employed 20,000 people (excluding the peace-keeping forces) in 1962: by 1982, this figure had grown to 50,721. In contrast, one estimate for the total number of people employed by international organizations before the Second World War put the figure at only 1,500.

Even more rapid has been the growth of non-governmental organizations (N.G.O.s), which had also begun to spring up during the nineteenth century. The first international conference of N.G.O.s was probably the world Anti-Slave Conference of 1840. N.G.O. is a term which covers a wide range of organizations with a remarkably varied list of goals and pursuits, ranging from associations of people with similar interests, whether they be in pigeons or in Japanese flower arranging, to those grouping sports clubs, educational bodies, etc., with representatives in every country and representation at governmental level; they can range from one dedicated organizer corresponding with members from his own home, to large secretariats.

These international organizations - both governmental and non-governmental - cluster in a relatively small number of cities. They include some of the larger capitals and smaller cities, such as Strasbourg, Geneva and Brussels. The last two were chosen as the headquarters of major international organizations for several reasons which include their central location in Europe, transport and communication facilities, the attitude of public authorities towards the establishment of international headquarters, financial and banking facilities, availability of office space and room for expansion. In the case of Geneva, traditional Swiss neutrality also played an important role.

In 1985, Geneva was host to 249 international organizations - 15 inter-governmental organizations, of which eight were part of the United Nations and included the U.N. itself, 106 non-governmental organizations, two permanent international commissions, three governmental organization representations and 123 permanent delegations - altogether about 22,000 people, representing 9% of the jobs in the entire canton of Geneva.

Brussels is also a good illustration of how a small city - in this case, the capital of a small country - can, in the space of twenty-five years, become a thriving international centre.

In 1960, there were 148 international organizations or institutions in Brussels. Ten years later, their number had multiplied to 392 and, a couple of years after that, they had reached the figure of 444. By 1981, they totalled nearly 600. Industrial and commercial companies dependent on, or affiliated to a multinational or foreign concern were subject to the same phenomenon: from 39 in 1959 they grew to 311 in 1965, to 1,220 in 1976, to 1,248 in 1980.

The effect of the presence of the E.C. on the population of Brussels was assessed in a study published in 1982; it showed that the number of foreigners living there as a result of this enormous international expansion, but excluding the staff of N.A.T.O., amounted to 100,000 out of a population of 1 million. [5]

****

Besides the international organizations, it would be hard to find more spectacular examples of organizations that move goods and people around the world than the multinationals. These vast, interlocked business empires may have their headquarters in Illinois, Minnesota or Chicago, in Tokyo, Brussels or London, but their affiliates and member companies are found throughout the world. 'It was once said that the sun never sets on the British Empire', remarked the President of the Worldwatch Committee. 'Today, the sun does set on the British Empire, but not on the scores of global, corporate empires. For the past few centuries, the world has been neatly divided into a set of independent, sovereign nation states. With the emergence of literally hundreds of multi-national or global corporations, the organization of the world into mutually exclusive political entities is now being overlaid by a network of economic institutions.' [6]

The Americans were the first to look overseas for expansion and, during the 1950s, their external direct investment rose from twenty billion dollars to sixty billion. Affiliates and branches of American corporations sprang up in Europe. Names like I.B.M., Ford, Procter and Gamble, 3M, and others, virtually became household words in the European capitals. By 1971, it was estimated that at least 10,000 companies based in non-communist, high-technology nations had branches abroad, and over two thousand had affiliates in six or more Western countries.

Their growth has been viewed with suspicion on the part of many historians, economists and journalists. They have been called 'mysterious giants without visible owners', 'a crucial new factor in the world system', 'a challenge to the nation state'. Whether such opinions are true or not, and whatever one may feel about them, multinationals are relevant here because they need employees willing to travel and live in different countries. ' There is emerging a new breed of international technocrats with its own nesting habits, patterns of migration and mating calls', wrote one observer of the European scene in the 1970s. [7] Philips, the Dutch conglo-merate, employs 345,000 people worldwide, of whom 50% are in Europe; I.B.M. has 12 companies in Europe with a total staff of 99,000; Shell has 160,000 employees worldwide, with 65,000 in Europe and 5,000 employees worldwide who are not locally hired.

It is rumoured that the numbers of international transfers are being cut because of the cost to employers. It is hard to draw conclusions, however, for although many multinationals do seem to be relying more on employees who are nationals of the host countries, others declare that they still need to transfer personnel from country to country either because of their special skills or -

especially true of American multinationals - because local personnel are not attuned to their own policies and ways of working.

****

There remain two other major groups of organizations that employ expatriates - the armed forces and the diplomatic services. (Mention must be made, however, of the thousands of people in other professions - journalists, teachers, researchers, experts and consultants, priests, independent business people and so on - who work abroad. Most of those who fall into this latter group will lack the infrastructure and support mechanisms provided by the major employers and will, consequently, have a very different experience of expatriate life.)

The number of people in the armed forces of the N.A.T.O. countries stationed in Europe is well over half a million. Together with families and with a substantial number of civilians who work on the bases, the staggering figure of about 1,000,000 people is reached, all living outside their own countries, many of them in barracks and compounds with their own hospitals, schools and cut-price shops.

Despite their huge numbers, members of the armed forces and their families are scarcely noticed by the civilian expatriate communities who view them as a different species. They mix relatively little, or not at all, with the local population and tend to live within their own tightly-knit communities.

By contrast, the diplomatic community is a more evident component of international life. The network of diplomatic representation throughout the world is extensive though the number of people employed is relatively small. The British diplomatic service, for instance, employs about 5,000 people, distributed between 133 missions and 89 subordinate posts.

Over the last few decades the character of diplomatic representation everywhere has changed. Career diplomats have been joined by representatives of other branches of the civil services. Moreover, the growth of international organizations has created its own diplomatic needs and the largest among them, such as the United Nations, the European Community, the O.E.C.D. or N.A.T.O., are entities with their own foreign delegations headed by ambassadors. A city such as Brussels thus sees her foreign delegations multiplied by three: one for the Court of the King of the Belgians, one for the European Community and one for N.A.T.O. In 1957, 51 countries had delegations to the E.C. In 1973, there were 83 and the number of diplomats was put at 435; by 1980, there were 113 delegations with diplomats numbering 625. In these latter representations, the proportion of non-career diplomats (i.e. staff drawn from home ministries rather than the foreign services) is usually higher than that of career diplomats: in the Portuguese representation to the E.C., for instance, they outnumber career diplomats by three to one.

In spite of the recognition of the importance of 'nomadic' populations, there are numerous difficulties involved in gathering statistics on expatriates. Official statistics do not, for instance, include members of the diplomatic services or the armed forces. They also fail to make a distinction between long-term and short-term foreign residents - some long-term residents may have entered a country originally as prospective immigrants and do not, therefore, fall within the scope of this book. Nor do statistics distinguish expatriates by profession. Nevertheless, some idea of the number of people working outside their home countries may be obtained from them.*

Figures and statistics are important, even though they fluctuate wildly and make dull reading. Here, they confirm the fact that international mobility is a reality of the twentieth century, determined by political and economic needs. What they do not show is what it means to the people involved to uproot themselves and their families, how this changes their lives and how they relate to a system which is, by its very nature, dependent upon their willingness to live away from home.

****
_____

*Living in France in 1982, for instance, were, among other nationalities, 17,740 Americans, 4,980 Canadians, 34,18 Britons, 13,980 Dutch and 43,480 Germans. In West Germany there were, in 1984, 87,300 Britons and Northern Irish, 6,000 Irish, 81,700 Americans, 5,400 Australians, 72,380 French, 18,360 Belgians, 12,850 Danes. In Denmark, in 1984, there were 8,020 Germans, 1,610 Canadians, and 12 Luxembourgers. In the United Kingdom, in 1983, there were 3,700 Germans, 1,800 French, 1,500 Dutch, 6,700 Americans, 30,000 Canadians. In Switzerland, in 1986, for a population of 6.5 million, there were nearly one million foreigners, among them 81,870 Germans, 48,900 French, 17,430 Britons, 11,100 Dutch, 29,410 Austrians, 10,120 Americans. Though it is a very small country, Belgium has, because of the importance of Brussels as the European capital, a proportionally very high number of foreign residents: in 1984, it boasted 27,450 Germans, 103,100 French, 65,580 Dutch, 22,290 Britons, 1,890 Danes, 1,110 Irish, 10,870 Americans and 1,480 Canadians. (All figures have been rounded off to the nearest nought.)

International mobility is characterized by three broad types of move, or transfer, each with its own distinctive traits and each, for the women who are the camp-followers, with its own advantages and disadvantages.

The first is the infrequent isolated, or 'one-off' move, an exceptional experience in a person's professional history which is usually of a specified length of time. The second is the repeated or frequent move which usually lasts from two to five years and is just one in a pattern of many. The third is the longer, indefinite or open-ended move which may, in the long run, become permanent.

Among those who are living abroad for a specified length of time and on an exceptional basis, may be found business executives, teachers and preachers, government officials 'on loan' to the foreign service, to foreign governments or international organi-sations, experts and consultants. In the second category, the recurrent movers are business executives - the 'corporate gipsies' - diplomats, specialists of various kinds, consultants, and journal-ists. In the third, are international civil servants working for organisations such as the E.C. or the U.N., others working for private or non-governmental organisations, some businessmen, and expatriates who have 'stayed on' to become residents abroad.

The first category of moves is generally experienced as the easiest to decide on and to live. Women often think of it as an extended holiday, a chance to get away from humdrum routines, to travel and to experience other cultures.

22% of the women in this book are living abroad on this basis. Yet, although of the three types of move this may be the the easiest to experience, it can still prove to be more difficult than originally imagined. Holiday feelings soon evaporate, husbands disappear to their offices, tourist activities pall unexpectedly quickly. Women who had greeted the offer to go abroad with relief - as time off from work - find that long vacations can become boring.

Accepting a move of a specific length of time is easier for women if they know their job will be kept open for them, or that they will be helped to find work upon their return. In the absence of such knowledge, they may become anxious about their future employ-ment and this may cast a shadow over their stay abroad. Women who are planning a family or are at home with small children are more likely to welcome and accept a move for a limited period than women who are concentrating on their career or whose children are at a critical stage in their development.

The second category of moves concerns 57% of the women in this study whose husbands have professions which demand constant mobility. These perpetually uprooted women express a definite ambivalence about their lives, for the quickening of interest they may feel at the thought of seeing yet another culture at close range is frequently offset by a weariness brought on by repeated disruption and the knowledge that they will never be in one place long enough to allow it to make a profound mark on them or to be able to make a mark on it; to develop and keep up friendships, to build a career; in short, to live with a certain sense of permanence.

Yet a paradoxical aspect of repeated versus permanent or open-ended moves - the third category, which concerns 21% of the women in this book - is that many of the women who are frequently transferred, particularly those married to men in the foreign services who spend periods of time on home postings, maintain close links with their home country, keeping a house there, or - this is particularly true of the British - sending their children back home to school both because it is a tradition in some circles and in order to avoid constant interruption in their education. This means that although these women may not develop close ties with their temporary place of residence, they have a clear idea of where their home is. They are not prey to the confusion which may beset a woman who has been living in a foreign country for a long time when, for instance, as her children grow older, decisions have to be taken about where they will have their post-school education and where they will work in the future. Confusion also emerges as retirement approaches and couples begin to wonder where they will live when the reasons for which they are abroad have gone.

Just as individual women differ, so do their experiences of mobility. Character and personal circumstances, the length and frequency of moves, the environment in which these take place, make each of these experiences unique, and the veins of similarity which run through them not only establish patterns but emphasize the uniqueness of each case.

One such pattern is provided by the disruption which a move to another country causes in the lives of people, however inured they may be to living like nomads. The element of continuity, the flowing and unfolding which tends to be present when sedentary people talk about their lives, is often missing when expatriate wives talk about theirs. Whoever they are, and whatever their feelings about their move or their way of life, their sense of continuity is impaired and the words they use express fragmentation, transience and unreality.

'This is a chunk out of my life', says one; 'I'm marking time and having babies till I can resume the thread of my life', says another. 'It's an interlude dominated by the longing to get home, to take up the reins of my life again', says a third. Others describe their lives abroad as 'living in parentheses', 'limbo', 'a period of reassessment', 'an adventure', 'an unreal experience', 'an escape', 'a passage from a book'.

[1] Brookner, Anita, *Hôtel du Lac*, London, 1984.
[2]. Morris, J., *Farewell the Trumpets: An Imperial Retreat*, Harmondsworth, 1979.
[3]. Whyte, William H., *The Organisation Man*, Harmondsworth, 1960.
[4]. Toffler, Alvin, *Future Shock*, New York, 1970.
[5]. Centre d'Etudes et de Recherches Urbaines, *L'Europe à Bruxelles*, Brussels, 1982.
[6]. Toffler, Alvin, *The Third Wave*, New York, 1980.
[7]. Sampson, Anthony, *The New Europeans*, London, 1968.

2

The Human Chessboard

The problem is not, therefore, to suppress change,
which cannot be done, but to manage it.

Alvin Toffler,
Future Shock, New York, 1970

The analogy of chess is hard to resist in relation to much-travelled expatriates. It neatly fits a picture of human pieces who, trailing their families and belongings behind them, move at the command of giant players across the countries of the world.

The policies adopted by employing organizations in relation to their expatriate employees display enormous variations in all areas. Take, for instance, the subject of salaries and 'perks'. Expatriates are widely believed to earn huge salaries and have luxurious 'perks' - large houses, chauffeur-driven cars, servants and generous entertainment allowances. In reality, although it is certainly true that many expatriates earn larger salaries than they would in their home countries, and that some of them benefit from special advantages, this is not the case for many others who must find their own housing, pay for their children's schooling themselves, run their own cars and live much as they would at home, sometimes in countries where the cost of living is higher than in their own.

Variations in calculating salaries are immense. Employers with a large work-force in foreign countries - like the multinationals - have worked out elaborate scales to calculate individual salaries, based on the cost of living in various places abroad, school fees, health care, and even the security risks involved in living in certain countries.

The nationality of employees may also play a part in determining their salaries. Many employers guarantee that the salary will be higher than an employee would be earning in his home country. As a result, a Swiss employee, for instance, holding the same job in the same country as a British or Belgian employee, could well be earning more than his colleagues because Swiss salaries are much higher than those in the United Kingdom or Belgium.

Most companies pay for all moving costs, arrange necessary documents and steer family and possessions through customs. Some go further, guaranteeing the lease on a house, helping their employees to find it and paying expensive school fees. Others go further still to compensate employees for going abroad - like one American company which stored their employees' furniture at home and paid for a master carpenter to build identical furniture for their new house. Such an inducement would be undreamed of for an employee in an international organization where the attitudes are quite different to those of the multinationals.

We think it useful to illustrate some of these disparities in policies and attitudes by examining the personnel policies of three of the major employers of expatriates - the multinationals, the foreign services and the international organizations.

The information presented here has been obtained both from staff and from wives, thus giving, we believe, a more balanced picture than if we had spoken only to the women.

.   **********

What is known as 'the transfer system' is vital to companies operating internationally. An executive may be transferred to another branch to train staff or to oversee a project, or the transfer may be offered as a means of acquiring training in a particular skill, or simply in order to get international experience, deemed essential by many companies. International transfers and promotion go hand in hand. 'We use the transfer system a great deal', said the personnel manager of a large multinational based in Brussels. 'It is good for the company and it is good for the individual. It allows him to grow, and the company benefits.'

The transfer system, however, is creaking under the strain caused by the employees themselves.

We talked to personnel managers and directors about the problems they were facing with their international staff and they responded, on the whole, with a certain amount of awareness of and sensitivity to the problems. Some proved to be particularly perceptive in identifying problem areas and outlining possible ways of alleviating them; and some openly critized their own management for misusing the transfer system. They believed that many transfers were unnecessary; that, at times, transfers were used by management as short-term solutions to problems with employees; that top management was often unaware of the upheaval and distress caused by transfers and particularly insensitive to the effects of recurrent moves on employees' families.

The problem which, to an increasing extent, is facing companies and other employers who demand mobility of their staff, is two-fold: on the one hand, more and more employees are turning down offers to work abroad; on the other, there is an increase in the number of employees who, once abroad, have to be repatriated before the end of their contract because they or their family are unable to cope with some of the strains arising from transplantation. The economic and structural problems this double phenomenon causes for employers are considerable.

Some of the reasons given by employees for turning down the offer
of a post abroad or which, later, could cause particular stress
during their term away from home, are the existence of aged
parents in their home country, children's education and,
increasingly, the question of wives' employment.

This last issue is a relatively new obstacle but one which is fast
moving to the front line. The figures for women's employment have
practically doubled in many Western countries over the last few
years and the wives of many potential expatriates are working and
often earning sizeable salaries. Not only do they not wish to give up
their jobs because of the personal satisfaction they derive from
them, but the increased salary usually offered to an employee going
abroad may not be high enough to compensate for the loss of a
wife's earnings. Moreover, going abroad may mean not just a
temporary setback to a woman's career but a permanent one which
can radically affect her future earning power.

The problems arising when employees who have moved abroad
with their families find themselves unable to adapt to life in their
host country, are often less concrete and, therefore, more difficult
to deal with. The failure of a transfer is expensive, both in human
terms for the employee and his family, and in financial terms for
the company. 'Companies neglect selection, briefing and support
of expatriates at their peril', reports one newspaper article, 'when
you consider that the cost of maintaining an expatriate is three
times their annual domestic salary'.[1]

Employers are increasingly aware that the success or failure of a
transfer depends not only on the employee but also on the success
of his family, particularly his wife, in adapting to life abroad.
Mobility has become an issue which forces companies to look at
their policies generally in regard to families. At one end of the scale
you have the point of view that home and work are totally different
areas of an employee's life and should be kept separated; at the
other, the belief that the spheres of work and home interact, and
that one will necessarily affect the other.

A British engineer working for a large multinational company
explained that his employers' lack of caring policies were 'the
product of a culture which says: "Whatever happens in your family
life is up to you to fix, and the company will not interfere. We're
going to be very generous in terms of financial and medical
assistance, but whatever happens in your private life is none of our
business. The only one who counts for us is you"'.

The opposite point of view was expressed by the personnel manager of a large American firm: 'I make a point of interviewing possible transferees and their wives myself,' he explained, 'first in the United States and then in Europe. When the couple come to Europe, my wife and I have dinner with them. We have our antennae out; we are looking at the husband-wife relationship. There is a certain school of thought', he continued, 'that says that a man's private life should have nothing to do with the company. But I believe it is very important.'

Company policy towards wives appears to have come a certain way in the last decade. The importance of wives as essential providers of back-up services has never been underestimated by management, but their well-being, personal fulfillment and individual goals were until recently largely ignored. In his book, *Anxiety of the Executive*, published in 1969, American psychiatrist Alan N. Schoonmaker commented: 'The company attitude is that a wife must move without complaint to wherever the corporation wants to send her husband, be cheerful and gracious when he brings home unexpected guests (even if she dislikes them), accept his long hours and company travel with a smile, run her house like a branch office, express the proper political and economic attitudes, drop her old friends as he moves up, and change her personality and habits, if necessary, to fit in with his job and associates. In other words, she is allowed to have no needs or personality of her own, because her husband's career is more important than she is.' [2]

Today companies are increasingly identifying problem areas and specific periods during which they may be called upon to give extra back-up services. But what practical and moral support are they actually giving their expatriate employees? And are they changing their policies to deal with new pressures, such as the problem of working wives?

Our enquiries showed enormous differences between companies in the degree of preparation given to families before they went to live abroad. Certain companies - all of them American - make sure that wives have a 'clear' picture of what to expect. This preparation may consist of a lecture, complete with film or video presentation showing tourist sights, the kind of housing available, possible schools for their children, and other aspects of the city they are going to. It may also include a more general talk on culture shock and hints on how best to deal with it. Language classes are sometimes provided before and after the move.

Some companies use outside organizations to provide employees and their families with information. In Britain, for instance, the

Centre for International Briefing at Farnham Castle, Surrey, founded in 1953, provides residential courses which cover major aspects of life in over seventy countries - most of them outside Europe. Similarly, the Women's Corona Society in London runs one-day briefing sessions with special rates for couples, to which certain British companies send their prospective expatriates.

Frequently, in place of this presentation, or in addition to it, wives and husbands are sent at company expense to their future host country. This sometimes occurs before the decision to accept a transfer has been made, and it forms part of the decision-making process. Or it may take place afterwards, and the trip then becomes primarily a house-hunting expedition.

A study made in the 1970s of multinational policies towards expatriates found that wives often acquired an exaggerated view of the advantages of going abroad because it was left to their husbands to pass on information. All the personnel managers we interviewed declared that they encouraged wives to approach them directly with questions. Nevertheless, it was clear that husbands were still the main channels of communication: it was through them that wives first heard of the impending transfer, and through them that wives' reactions were reported to the company.

The support given by companies to newly-arriving families varies greatly in kind and length. Some companies assign specially trained staff to show wives houses, schools and areas, and supply information ranging from the type of flour or meat cuts available to the history and culture of the country. Others rely on 'a sort of stepmother and stepfather system', as one executive described it, by which other employees who are familiar with the host country act as sponsors, making sure 'that doors are opened and mistakes forestalled'.

The importance of preparation and briefing was underlined by personnel staff who were sometimes well aware that what their own companies were providing was insufficient. One woman manager, herself an expatriate wife, said of her firm - rated as one of the best in the level of information it gave to employees - that she was aware of one significant gap in their policy. 'We should', she said, 'prepare people more before the job is accepted. We should be pointing out to the family the possible problems they are going to encounter. In effect, this advice is usually given during the house-hunting trip and *after* the decision to go has been taken. Families themselves have to make the decision of whether or not to accept a transfer, and a decision not to go must be respected. You have to rely on the strength and maturity of people themselves for that decision, but very often I don't think that they are aware of the potential difficulties and that is where we fall down.'

****

We asked personnel managers how their companies responded to wives who wished to work. 'There is much more openness in my company now about the problem of wives and work than there has been in the past,' declared the manager of a large American company, echoing what certain other managers had told us. 'We cannot guarantee or create work for wives, but whenever the opportunity arises, we should and must use it to help wives whose husbands are being transferred.' In practical terms, this means that certain companies have relaxed their hitherto inflexible rules about employing both husband and wife, and are now prepared to hire wives as long as they do not work directly with their husbands.

An article in *The International Herald Tribune*, dated 24 July 1986, described the difficulties of obtaining work permits for expatriate spouses and reported that, although in the United States, some companies were offering help in finding jobs for the spouses of relocated employees, most American companies let the wives of executives moving overseas 'fend for themselves', because of difficulties with immigration laws.

Obtaining work permits for those who need them was acknowledged by companies to be a difficult task. Most declared their willingness to contact employment agencies, send *curriculum vitae* and help in an informal way to find work for spouses, but few were prepared to go further.

The company's responsibility in presenting future expatriates with a realistic picture of the difficulties for wives in obtaining work abroad was underlined by one member of personnel management we spoke to. False expectations about the foreign labour market, the let-down when, on arrival, a woman discovers she cannot be employed could sour the whole experience of being abroad. It was, this executive felt, the company's responsibility to present a realistic picture so that the possibility of not being able to work could be understood and accepted before arrival in the new country.

One 'solution' to the problem of working wives was given by the personnel director of a Belgium-based multinational. 'Previously,' he said, 'we used to send experienced people abroad. Now we take a risk and send young employees, because a young wife can adapt more easily to the idea. I believe', he emphasized, 'that this is the thing to do - send couples abroad much earlier so that the wife will only have been working for one or two years. She will not have had time to get very far in her career, and she will find it easier to give it up.'

No other company we spoke to had explicitly adopted this solution which, it is clear, may be one way to avoid employees' refusals to go abroad, but which may not help a woman when, upon her return to her home country, she has to reinsert herself in the labour market several years later than her contemporaries. On the other hand, being abroad in the early years of a marriage may actually suit a lot of women and fit in with plans to have children and not be employed while they are small.

****

Some of the more enlightened personnel managers were also concerned with the long-term problems of mobility since these, too, are increasingly becoming reasons for the refusal of transfers. An example of such an issue is the disturbing effect that frequent uprooting may have on children. Another is the situation of women whose grown-up children have left home, and who are suffering from depression, isolation, and too much time on their hands. This, of course, is a problem faced by women both in their own countries and abroad, and solutions are difficult to find in all cases. Living in a foreign country only emphasizes the problem.

Of all international cities, Brussels is possibly the best organized in terms of support for its large international community: there are, for instance, several counselling centres providing therapy of various kinds in different languages. Much of the financial support for these centres comes from the business world. One large multinational is even considering the presence of specialized counsellors within its own medical service, on the lines of many American companies in the United States.

Wives' associations and organized social functions are put forward by companies as support mechanisms for women abroad. Conferences, too, often include wives, although this is usually limited to the social dimension of the organized schedule. Sometimes, in an attempt to lessen the gap between work and home, special presentations are given on different aspects of company business, and wives and husbands are brought together in seminars on subjects of common interest or of particular sensitivity to family life.

****

Women's views on the same questions fell into several patterns: some wives were appreciative of company personnel policy; some felt that, as far as the company was concerned, they did not exist; others in the same category were relieved to be free to do as they pleased. Others still were scornful of company pretensions of caring for wives' well-being, which the women felt to be in reality efforts at appeasement - a way of 'buying off' potentially difficult wives. These women expressed a definite cynicism about any revision on the part of corporations and multinationals of the basic role they expected employees' wives to play. As far as they were concerned, the basic do's and dont's laid down traditionally for the behaviour of wives, still held true, though they were perhaps less overtly expressed than in the past.

Judith Greber's novel about a corporation wife, *The Silent Partner,* leaves one in no doubt that even in the mid-1980s the traditional role and pressures 'trailing wives' are subject to had still not changed in some corporations: 'A good corporate wife never complained. She was a chameleon, moving from subtropics to near-arctic, from metropolis to backwater, blending her hues with whatever local color was offered. She never told other corporate wives that she minded the process or found it difficult because they had corporation husbands who would be interested by the information. Nobody wanted to move a whiner into another town where she'd spread bad will and a poor company image.' [3]

On the subject of refusing a transfer, wives on the whole doubted employers' claims that their husbands would not be penalized. One American woman, whose highly lucrative career was the reason for which her husband had refused to move, was convinced that his career had been blocked as a result. Another said that, years after her husband had turned down a transfer for family reasons, his refusal was referred to in a meeting. She felt she had been labelled a 'difficult wife'.

As to the way in which the transfer offer was communicated, only one wife - who herself had an important and highly-paid job - said that she had participated in the initial discussions about the possibility of a transfer abroad. 'The company', she related, 'flew their personnel staff to us - we happened to be on holiday at the time - and talked to us about whether we wanted to accept this position.'

For all the other women, the news of their transfer was announced by their husbands. Greta, a Swede, who had moved from place to place for short periods of time, described how her husband's boss reacted to his consternation at being told of the imminence of another move so soon after the last. 'What shall I tell my wife?' her husband said. 'She didn't want to come here in the first place.' 'Well', was the reply, 'you'd better tell her she was right in the first place.'

Briefing on the part of the company ranged from the careful to the minimal. Among the former, perhaps none was more elaborate than that given to an American wife, Lana, and her family before she and her husband were flown to Belgium on a house-hunting trip. 'They sent us for several days to a place in Colorado for a workshop which they had organized just for the family. We had films about Belgium and lectures by a specialist on its history and culture, as well as a talk about culture shock. Even the children were briefed by a teacher about what to expect and they were taught some French and Dutch words.'

More typical of the run-of-the-mill experience was Lettie's, another American. 'I had a week for house hunting before moving. Apart from dinner with the president and his wife, it was left to me to find my way around. I picked up whatever information I could from the American Women's Association.'

While personnel managers had told us that normally a period of about two months was calculated to be sufficient between the moment an employee was informed of his transfer and his actual departure, in practice the period is often much shorter. This was a subject on which many women had strong feelings. An American told us that her husband's boss had been given just one day to move, although his wife was due to have a baby the following week. Similarly, an Australian woman told us her husband had been given two days' notice on a transfer. 'We'd only been there three months, but it was what I'd come to expect. I'd be totally amazed if I knew where I'd be in the next three months.'

****

In contrast to the multinationals' hesitation, the foreign services have always incorporated wives into their structure. They have, in the past, taken it for granted that they were getting two employees for the price of one. Traditionally much diplomacy was, if not actually conducted at the dinner table, certainly helped along by good food and wine and a gracious atmosphere. The duties that in many foreign services are still expected justify the claim that to be a diplomat's wife can be a career in itself.

The higher her husband's grade, the more is expected of the diplomatic wife. Traditionally, specific officers' wives have specific duties: the Head of Chancery's wife in the British Diplomatic Service, for example, is responsible for family welfare in the embassy. Although the official attitude is that British diplomatic wives are 'under no contractual obligation' to carry out any embassy duties, it was reported that one ambassador in a difficult post had refused to take as his Head of Chancery anyone who was unmarried or whose wife would not accept responsibility for family welfare.

The suitability of wives can still affect their husbands' careers. Until the 1970s, it was a known fact that the American Foreign Service prepared reports on spouses. Almost certainly, some kind of scrutiny of wives still goes on in most diplomatic services. It is felt that a woman can hinder her husband's career and perhaps block it by her conduct, although the canons of what constitutes 'seemly' or 'unseemly' behaviour have surely changed somewhat in the last decade.

If the diplomat's wife has a role which is acknowledged by her husband's employer, what is provided in return for her services?

The answer would have been clearer in the past than it is in the present. For many wives, it may still be that their reward lies in feeling 'part of the show', as one woman expressed it, in feeling that they have a role to play not only in helping their husbands, but in helping their country. The recognition of this role is active involvement via social duties.

Many diplomats' wives told us that they had enjoyed the 'hardship' or difficult posts, where the conditions were apparently so much less attractive than those in sophisticated European capitals, because of the closeness of the community and because of the role they were called upon to play.

'Work' satisfaction may be one answer, therefore, to the question of reward. Prestige is another. And financial compensation yet another, for postings abroad are rewarded by higher salaries and other advantages. The 'perks' of diplomatic life are legendary: free housing, entertainment allowance, children's schooling, are taken for granted, though, of course, these do not apply to all grades. Getting to know other countries and meeting people one might not otherwise have met are further attractions to many wives.

Diplomatic services generally provide for their employees' families in a way that other employing organizations do not, although the extent varies from one service to the other and is subject to size and tradition. Certainly the larger services provide for their incoming employees amenities of a magnitude unknown to other expatriate families. Accommodation, probably furnished, awaits them and is consistent with the status of the employee. Its size and luxuriousness depend on his grade and the amount of entertaining he is expected to do. The practical details of the actual move and all the paperwork are dealt with by the office, and there is always an official to help wives with information, ranging from buying cars or washing machines to who's who in the diplomatic world and how they should be seated at the dinner table. It should be pointed out that this is how some foreign services function in some places; others do not necessarily provide the soft cushion for families that this picture suggests.

But, if all foreign services provide some kind of back-up structure for wives, there is usually little official help in preparing families for life abroad. As is the case with large companies, the Americans are the most thorough in the formal preparation they give diplomats' wives. At the Overseas Briefing Centre in Washington, wives go to courses ranging from how to prepare elaborate menus and organize formal dinners to detailed analyses of what they are likely to feel - the famous culture shock - on arrival in a new country.

Diplomats' wives from other countries were, on the whole astonished to hear of this kind of preparation. Many had had access to language courses and, occasionally, to courses on international relations. Their usual form of preparation consisted of the circulation of 'post reports' - accounts written by outgoing diplomats on the general conditions of the host country, its customs, political situation, culture, and so on. These could include reports prepared by the wives of these diplomats fo the benefit of their incoming counterparts.

The foreign service, however, like other prese .t-day institutio.~s, is increasingly prey to the changes which 'iavr taken place in the economic status and social structure of Western industrialized countries. The changed role of worr en i i society is reflected in the attitude of foreign service wives.

As in other professions which involve mobility, strain on the system is being caused by wives who are no longer willing to move from one part of the world to another, but want to have their own professions. The number of divorces in the foreign services is said to be rising and the number of suitable applicants willing to travel, diminishing. The statement we heard from one Dutch diplomat's wife that the difference between diplomats' wives who remained married and those who divorced was that one group did not want to work while the other did, is no doubt extreme but reflects the tension of wives caught between marital duties and personal goals.

Foreign services react to this situation in very different ways. In order to cope with wives' changes in attitude, some have changed their own. The Danish Ministry of Foreign Affairs positively encourages ambassadors to help wives find work abroad, and when a Danish diplomat returns home, his wife may be helped to get a job in Denmark. Several Danish women told us that no pressure was put on them to accompany their husbands on a posting and that, indeed, many stay at home to pursue their own careers.

Other foreign services still formally forbid their diplomats' wives to work or discourage them, as is the case, among others, of the Belgian, Luxembourg, Dutch and Portuguese foreign services. For others permission must be sought from the ambassador. Many services make it clear that, if wives do hold jobs, their work must not interfere with the duties expected of them as diplomats' wives.

The cohesiveness of diplomatic life is itself a strength that can be utilised by wives. Many services have active wives' associations that have served in recent years as channels to voice problems and issues. An official sign of the importance of these associations is the growing number of foreign services which allot them office space and pay their staffs' salaries. The magazines they produce deal increasingly with subjects of contention: What is the role of a diplomat's wife? What is the exact nature of her duties? What other work can she train for that will fit in with her nomadic life? And what, moreover, are the other diplomatic services doing in response to pressure from wives?

Some foreign service wives have voiced the opinion that the answer to the conflict between embassy duties and personal work lies in a system of financial remuneration - in other words, they suggest that, in addition to their husbands' salary, their country should also pay them for what they do on its behalf. There are a few services - some from Asia, for instance - that do provide payment for wives. American wives have been campaigning for some time to be paid for their entertainment duties, but the subject arouses strong feelings both for and against, and, at the time of writing, there was little sign of any settlement.

The Americans formally recognized the role of diplomats' wives in welfare work in 1972 by declaring that they were no longer under any obligation to perform welfare functions. As wives opted out, a gap was left in the welfare services of embassies and, gradually, family or community liaison officers were appointed in their place.

Many foreign services do not give diplomatic wives the right to claim any part of their husbands' occupational pension - a fact that rouses much bitterness among wives who feel that they have sacrificed their own professions because of the constant travelling and spent much time supporting those of their husbands. Recognition of the 'sacrifice' that diplomats' wives make for their husbands' careers has, indeed, brought some foreign services - notably the Scandinavian countries - to provide pensions for divorced wives as well as widows.

The changing conditions of diplomatic life - whether in terms of prestige and 'perks' or job satisfaction - were evoked by one British diplomat's wife we spoke to. 'I think times have changed', she said. 'In the old days you felt more part of the show. There's a general feeling now that you're only the person who makes the wheels go round. You're the one who makes sure that your husband's clothes are in order, that the dinner is on the table; but you're less and less the person who contributes to your husband's career by being well-informed about the politics of the country you are in. You're more and more a factotum. I'm really beginning to wonder just how important I really am to the foreign service and, in fact, to my husband.'

****

There is a vast difference in attitude towards employees and their families between the two categories of employers we have just looked at - the multinationals and the foreign services - and the international organizations.

Many of the international organizations have an impressive array of facilities which employees' families can use. The Commission of the European Communities, for instance, with a staff of between eight and nine thousand based in Brussels alone, has sporting complexes, various leisure and cultural clubs and circles, an information centre, medical and social services and two schools set up especially for the children of employees.

Newcomers to the Commission receive a thick booklet describing these facilities and services, and details of housing are available at the information centre. But any more personal approach, any particular support for families at the moment of arrival, is absent.

There is also the problem of wives' work. Many of the international organizations have strict rules forbidding the employment of spouses. This is the case of U.N.E.S.C.O. in Paris, and since under French law non-E.C. residents have no right to work in France many of the wives and children of U.N.E.S.C.O. officials have no chance of employment at all. Although staff of international organizations are hired on a permanent basis, it seems to be assumed that should the husband die the wife and her family will return to their native country, however long it may be since they left and however hard it may be to find work there. At a one-day conference run by the Community Service in 1984 the insecurity of the expatriate wives surfaced, and the one question that roused universal concern was about the future of widows should their husbands die while employed by U.N.E.S.C.O.

A spokesman for one of the biggest international organizations said candidly that he realized his organization's personnel policies were, in many ways, far less humane than those that might be found in industry. Business needs made industry care more for its employees, while international organizations felt they could afford to have a 'take it or leave it' attitude.

Not everyone is as unsympathetic to the personal situation of these international expatriates. The conclusion of a report on international civil servants for the International Labour Organization in Geneva looked at expatriates with deeper understanding. 'Leaving one's own country,' says the author, 'is the sacrifice of something fundamental and irreplaceable, of being an organic part composed of history, politics, a broad spectrum of society, citizenship rights, etc. One exchanges these for another society which is narrowly composed, a huge bureaucracy artificially grafted onto a background... in which one cannot play a full role.' [4]

What makes a considerable difference between being an international civil servant and being a diplomat is that employees of the former, despite their quasi-diplomatic status, are not considered to be on foreign postings; neither are they considered to be likely to move on after a certain period of time. Both these factors make for a fundamentally different approach from their employers.

How do wives feel about the *laissez-faire* attitude of the
international organizations for which their husbands work? The
answer depends on the kind of woman she is and how long she has
been abroad. We put the question to several women whose
husbands had worked for both a foreign service and an
international organization. None of them had any hesitation about
which they would choose, were they given the choice again. One
said: 'In contrast to the diplomatic house we now live in, we lived
in a small flat. We had none of the perks of the foreign service. We
just had Bill's pay. I did so much more work - of my own - I mean
- I had no entertaining to do. I'd rather have that.' The others
agreed.

Having listed her past assets as a diplomat's wife, one of these
women concluded: 'In the long term, I would prefer to be as I am
now. You are, at least, your own person.'

[1]. *The Economist*, 3 March 1984.
[2]. Schoonmaker, Alan N., *Anxiety of the Executive*, New York, 1969.
[3]. Greber, Judith, *The Silent Partner*, London, 1985.
[4]. Flagstaffe, N., quoted in Geneva Women's Cooperative, *op.cit.*

3

All This But Not Enough

But no, I will not lay me down.

Robert Graves,
Leaving the Rest Unsaid, from *Collected Poems*, 1959

'The delegates came in, laughing and talking. What an extraordi-
nary attractive lot they were! Such a collection of many-coloured,
multi-nationed men and women would be what a film-producer
would try to shoot to make a scene from some idealized picture of
united nations. But would the actors have been able to convey such
a perfection of casual authority, such assurance?

'... Outside this great public building the conflicts went on. But
here? Had these easy well-tuned creatures, each burnished and
polished by money ever suffered? Ever wept in the dark? Ever
wanted something they could not get? Of course they had, they
must have, but there was no sign of it'.[1]

Our latter-day nomads, 'burnished and polished by money', are a
far cry from the seedy, alcoholic, self-loathing expatriates familiar
to readers of Joseph Conrad, Somerset Maugham, Graham Greene
or Malcolm Lowry. It must nevertheless be obvious to our readers
by now that there is a darker underside to the image of the gilded
expatriate life: reality has caught up with the myth. (The myth
itself, if the data gathered from our sample of expatriates is
anything to go by, was a mere illusion to start with: just over half
(53%) of the respondents said they had a higher standard of living
abroad than they did at home.)

But although the situation and problems described by newspaper
reports are doubtless accurate and were confirmed not only by
psychologists, psychiatrists, management personnel and foreign
service officials but more directly, by many of the women in our
study - we must stress that it is only one part of the picture. A more
global view of the situation of expatriates should take into
consideration all those men and women who are on the whole
content or coping satisfactorily with the way of life imposed upon
them by the demands of international mobility.

In our study, as many as 50% declared themselves reasonably
satisfied with their lives, while 36% expressed strongly negative
feelings and 14% hovered in between. As many as 84% of the
women declared their husbands to be satisfied with their jobs.

Even if one allowed for a certain amount of image-preserving in the
questionnaire answers, these figures and others relating to
generally positive feelings towards mobility are nevertheless high
and must be taken into consideration when one examines and
questions what has come to be known to media, psychologists and
employers alike as 'The Expatriate Situation'.

As we explained in Part II of this book, if the data sample provided by our questionnaires is representative of all areas of expatriate life in Europe and of all types of attitudes on the part of the women concerned, our study itself and our own approach to it are coloured particularly by the testimonies of women who tended to question aspects of their lives as expatriates. These were the women who came forward when news of our project appeared, who asked to be heard, advanced opinions, voiced conflicts and wished to discuss with others issues related to their situation.

It is not our intention to recap here all the issues these women raised but to single out the most significant and try to set them against the wider background of their situation and the data we gathered.

****

'How different would my life have been had I remained at home?'

This question that probably all expatriates, men and women, all over the world, ask themselves from time to time is, where some women are concerned, a recurrent one, a sort of leitmotiv that keeps open a constant comparison between their life abroad and what they imagine it might have been had they not taken the risk of following their husbands to other countries. For a risk it is, and as with all risk-taking, it pays off for some and not - or less - for others.

To that very question in their questionnaires, 76% of the women answered that they thought their life would have been very different had they stayed in their own countries; 15% felt that it might have been more or less similar, and 9% found it difficult to evaluate, usually because they had been away from home too long.

Of the 76% that answered 'very' and qualified their answers, 50% felt that the comparison weighed more heavily in favour of life at home. Almost all invoked, as their reason, the fact that at home they would have been working and moving up in their career. Many also thought that the quality of life at home would have been better, with closer friends, family, a system of reference they could relate to, a social and political context they could get involved with, and so on, even though some of them mentioned the fact that their actual standard of living would be lower.

The remaining 26%, on the other hand, felt that, in comparison with their life abroad, their life at home would have been duller, more routine-bound and far less comfortable financially and in terms of lifestyle. Some admitted that they felt happier to be away from family pressures; others, who had been isolated in their own country, were comforted by the fact that in an international community other people are in the same position as oneself. Almost all the 26% said that they found life far more stimulating than at home because of the challenge of discovering new countries and cultures and making friends of different nationalities.

It is hardly surprising, given the importance to expatriate wives of the subject of their own careers and employment that, of the 50% who thought that their lives would have been better had they stayed at home, almost all gave as their main reason the fact that in their own countries they would be working.

Indeed, the single most important concrete issue to have emerged from this study is the question of wives' work. It is obvious, also, that, from the point of view of employers, this is fast becoming the greatest obstacle to the mobility of families everywhere.

Unlike other problems caused or emphasized by the process of mobility and which are diffuse or entangled in psychological conflict, the subject of women's employment, an emotional issue though it undoubtedly is to many, is nevertheless relatively concrete and straightforward - which is perhaps one reason why so many people on either side of the fence focus so readily on it.

58% of the women in our sample had been employed in their own countries prior to going abroad. 81% of these worked, or expressed the wish to work in their host country. Those who found they could not, either because legislation forbade it, or because they had language or circumstantial problems, or simply because they could not find an outlet for their kind of career or qualifications, felt that the loss of their jobs was a continuous source of unhappiness, frustration and conflict to them.

Those who, in their own countries, had not been employed or had given up their jobs upon starting a family - 42% altogether - were mitigated in their responses, though two slight trends emerged: one of these showed that a number of younger women intended to seek employment at some point in the near-to-middle-term future; the other showed a stirring towards job-seeking on the part of wives who, having gone to live abroad when young and remained fulltime housewives and mothers, now found themselves in the situation where their children had left home and wanted to find some meaningful professional activity. Most of these women, however, expressed frustration at the scanty possibilities they found on foreign employment markets.

The question of work, then, has emerged as a vital issue in mobility both in the questionnaires that were sent back to us and in what women said in interviews and group discussions. It was a subject to which they returned time and time again. Many of the points they raised might have been raised in similar conversations with women living in their own countries. But the difference, it seems to us, is that many of the difficulties that women face anywhere are, as far as expatriate women are concerned, vastly multiplied and magnified by their being abroad, and that many of the options they might have had in their own countries are closed off.

****

Another issue that provoked strong reactions on the part of women was the effect of mobility on family relationships.

We had read in newspaper reports, before we had fully embarked on our project, that the stress of living abroad was responsible for a number of marriage breakdowns and divorces among expatriates. This was later confirmed by psychologists and counsellors to whom we talked and some of the women who came to group discussions, though we ourselves found it impossible for a number of reasons to evaluate the proportion of marital break-downs and divorces within our questionnaire data.

If there is one point on which the women who talked to us were virtually unanimous, it is that moves abroad are, like other important events in people's lives, physical and psychological upheavals which cannot but affect, if only temporarily, family relationships - more especially marital relationships. Like other important events also, moves and indeed the whole process of mobility are a catalyst that brings out certain traits of character and personality in individuals, irons out others and brings strains of its own, widening cracks already existing in relationships, or, on the contrary, consolidating relationships that are already strong.

We stressed several times already that the women who came to talk to us were mostly women who questioned aspects of their lives as expatriates. This may explain why their consensus in the opinion that mobility affects personal, particularly marital, relationships was not quite reflected in the data we obtained from our question-naires.

There, 28% of the respondents answered that their marital relationships had been virtually unaltered by their moves. 6%

declined to answer questions relating to personal relationships
and 3% found it difficult to express themselves on the subject. Of
the 63% who felt that their marital relationships had been altered
by mobility, 32% thought the effects had been positive while 31%
thought the contrary.

The reasons given by the former endorse Alvin Toffler's view that
mobility brings families closer together. They include, in order of
importance, mutual support under difficult conditions, greater
closeness brought about by the family's isolation in a foreign
country; the fact that some couples found they had more time to
do things together in their host country than at home and derived
greater enjoyment from their leisure activities; the ripening of each
partner brought about by the experience of mobility and the
reappraisal of personal relationships.

It is, needless to say, the very opposite picture we get from the other
31%. The reasons invoked here, again in order of importance,
include: husbands' greater involvement in their work, greater
tiredness and irritability, lesser availability to their families (one
woman described her husband as 'eccentric, intolerant, nervous,
he has become an outsider for his family, he has no time for us any
longer'; another wrote, 'he has changed beyond recognition, he is
drained of all enthusiasm for life, has no humour, is biased,
judgemental, stuffy, pompous and a role-player where once he was
none of this'); husbands' lack of understanding of their wives'
problems; the pressures of life abroad; lack of time to enjoy life
together; wives' greater dependence on their husbands, which
contributes to both their own resentment and their husbands'
irritability (in a few cases it was the opposite that caused a marital
rift: the wife's greater autonomy, gained through finding a professional activity and friends of her own, posed a problem for the
husband and changed the balance within the relationship).

****

If two of the main functions of the family are socialization and
emotional maintenance, when one lives in one's own country,
these functions are fulfilled by the combined inner and outer family
circles, with back-up services provided by the familiar culture and
environment. In mobility, however, the inner circle alone must be
relied on to provide its members with all the nurturing and
socialization they need.

In this way, then, the family in mobility may be said to undergo a process of nuclearization: it becomes a self-contained little bubble, floating about among countless other self-contained bubbles. This is not, however, the only kind of nuclearization that affects the family in mobility. Sociologically, a large percentage of mobile families, whatever their family pattern was originally, adopt or revert to a nuclear-family pattern in the traditional sense: consisting, that is, of a breadwinning father, a housekeeping, childminding mother, and one to three offspring.

This sociological nuclearization of the family in mobility - and in international mobility in particular, where the family is geographically even further away from the extended family - runs counter to the general trend in Western society in the last twenty-five years or so, a trend that has seen an overwhelming movement out of the nuclear-family pattern and into other family lifestyles. These not only include 'alternative' family patterns, such as commune-type families and so on, but, increasingly, dual-career families and single-parent households. The United States Department of Labor, for instance, in a report on marital and family characteristics in 1976, stated that only 7% of the entire population of the United States were living in a traditional nuclear-family pattern, and in recent years the figure has dropped even further.

The contrast between this trend and our own findings could not be more eloquent: 42% of the women in our study had, as expatriates, a nuclear-family pattern. The rest included dual-career families, families with more than three children, childless couples, commune-type families and extended families - the last two being extremely rare among the kind of expatriates this book has been dealing with, but nevertheless represented in our sample. (We included in the relevant categories women who followed their husbands abroad but have since divorced; and have put wives with part-time or voluntary work within the nuclear-family group for economic reasons.)

It seems evident from this that, although it runs counter to the trend in Western societies to diversify family patterns, the nuclear family is both a logical outcome of mobility and the ideal self-contained unit for employers to move around.

Beyond the fact that most women missed the extended family support structure, the most frustrating effect of the family's nuclearization in mobility was felt to be that the situation polarized gender roles within the household, accentuating the traditional role attribution and status hierarchy that are part of the classic family pattern anywhere, with the husband as breadwinner and giver of social status, and the wife as homemaker, nurturer and stabilizer.

This was felt by many of the women who talked to us to be a dangerously regressive trend, not only because it went against social progress and made a mockery of some of the gains the women's movement had fought so hard to achieve, but also because it put them at odds with most of their contemporaries at home and ill-prepared them for an eventual return to a quite different social context in their own country.

'It's like going back to the Dark Ages,' said Sally, an American lawyer, married to a medical expert 'on loan' to an international organization in Paris. 'All those years of struggling towards a more equal way of being together seem to have come to nothing. We're back to Square One.'

In the case of Sally and her husband, Don, the couple did not have any children. In the United States, where both had been employed in high-powered jobs, they had been accustomed to sharing most household tasks. When they went to Europe on a two-year contract for Don, Sally found that the work-permit situation and the shortness of their stay did not warrant her looking very hard for a job, so she did as many other women in her situation do, and decided to use her time abroad to catch up on reading and other interests.

For a while these activities sustained her. But what she was not prepared for was the speed with which she and Don slid into a totally alien pattern of life, in which he busied himself entirely outside the home and she busied herself entirely inside it. Nor was she prepared for the lethargy that came over her and prevented her from reacting against the pattern she perceived.

It was not only their sphere of activity that was different now, it was their territory as well. Before their move they had a common territory in their home. But now that she was at home all day, the Paris apartment and the kitchen in particular became her territory, and they both felt it - which only increased the distance and inequality that had developed between them. For Sally, as for many women, the sharing of traditionally feminine tasks with a husband is only acceptable if the woman has a full-time job.

The danger, in this situation which is only too common among expatriates, is not just that couples are compelled by the circumstances of their lives abroad to redefine their roles in a way that many women feel to be regressive, but also that the women themselves are caught up in a situation in which they find it hard - like Sally - to resist the pattern according to which they were socialized in the first place - a pattern that says that a wife must support her husband's work by providing physical and emotional nurturance, in return for which he will provide materially for the home; a pattern that also says, by extension, that a wife will put her own wishes and priorities second to her husband's. On a circumstantial level, the redefining of many expatriate couples' roles and spheres of activities comes not only from the fact that a number of wives find themselves jobless and housebound upon going to a new country, but also that their husbands' professions often entail extensive travelling. Many international businessmen or civil servants working for international organizations are away from home, sometimes as much as two to three weeks per month. Some live in a different city, sometimes even a different country, and join their wives and children at week-ends. There are others still whose travelling may be more limited, but whose professions or positions demand great involvement on their part, leaving them with little physical or emotional availability to their families.

This is where the woman's role in mobility takes on its full load of responsibility. As virtually a single parent and the only immediate object of reference to her children, the 'isolated matriarch', as she is known to sociologists, carries an enormous burden. Her moods, her sense of belonging, her rootlessness, her homesickness are, like her well-being, transmitted to her children, who react accordingly.

As with the effects of mobility on personal relationships, there was within the subject of expatriate children one point on which the women who talked to us were virtually unanimous, namely that their children's reactions to mobility were inevitably directly or indirectly affected by the way they themselves felt and behaved.

Whereas women seemed on the whole quite clear-sighted when talking or writing about the way in which mobility had affected their marital relationships, they appeared much less so where their children were concerned; partly, of course, because they often had no way of assessing the middle-to-long-term effects of mobility on their progeny; and partly because the whole subject was fraught with guilt.

We strongly felt, after many of the statements we heard, that parental guilt was a major concern in the problems of expatriate wives and that until some form of coming to terms with the subject was achieved, more parents, among future generations of expatriates, would be suffering from similar pangs and more children would be burdened by them. Central to the question is possibly the fact that, as social values change more slowly than social reality, we - the new nomads - are still nurturing notions of roots and belonging that, though comforting and real to many, are nevertheless values that have undergone a drastic upheaval in the last few decades and that are perhaps already part of a myth. Although we intellectually and verbally recognize the part we are playing in the social phenomenon of international mobility, we have not as yet internalized the implication of change it carries with it. We move from country to country because we accept the idea that it is an aspect of today's world and, even more so, of tomorrow's world, but we baulk internally at uprooting our children. We lament the distance that separates them from the rest of their family and fear they will grow up rootless and lost, with no sense of place or belonging. And we are forever on the lookout for signs that we have trespassed our rights as parents and caused them irreparable harm.

Parental guilt and anxiety among expatriates seem to have two main focuses - one that has to do with the experience of separation, transience and adaptation to an alien culture and the other that concerns cultural identity and the problem of rootlessness. As with other issues that preoccupy expatriates, this one, when broached in group discussions, was subject to conflict and controversy, out of which emerged at least one clear pattern. For want of a better word, we might term this the 'link' function of expatriate mothers, which consists of providing their children not only with continuity in a lifestyle marked by disruption, but also with a series of links: links between them and the relatives and friends who have been left behind and who, with time and distance, may grow shadowy in children's memories; links between the culture they belong to and the new culture they live in; links between one place that has left its mark upon them and another place that will also leave a mark.

This function has long been part of woman's role, not only in our Western culture, but in other cultures also. 'Woman', writes the French sociologist Evelyne Sullerot, 'is always represented as the mediator between the past and the present, while man sees himself as the mediator between the present and the future'.[2] Except that here, what expatriate women do is to mediate, for their children's sake, between the past, the present and the future.

---

[1] Lessing, Doris, *The Summer Before the Dark,* London, 1973.
[2] Sullerot, E., *Women, Society and Change,* New York, 1974.

4

The Face in the Mirror

I have crossed an ocean
I have lost my tongue,
from the root of the old one
a new one has sprung

Grace Nichols
Epilogue, from *The Fat Black Woman's Poems*,
London, 1984

During the preliminary discussions for this project, five women, including the authors of this book, spent a working week-end in an old millhouse in a remote corner of the Belgian Ardennes. Towards the end of the week-end, after we had listened to hours of taped interviews and had started to identify the themes that were emerging from them, one of us, relating her own experience of mobility, described how one morning, a few months after her arrival in Belgium, she had looked at herself in the mirror and had found, to her dismay, that she could not recognize the face that was staring back at her.

Instantly, two other women in the group, sprang up and said that they, too, had had the very same experience. And since then, other expatriate wives have echoed it, sometimes verbatim, sometimes with variations, but always describing a most disturbing feeling of disembodiment and disconnection from self.

Listen to Clara, a British journalist, married to a B.B.C. foreign correspondent: 'I found one day', she said, 'that I only had half a face. There was obviously some kind of terrible neurosis going on in my mind. And it had to do with moving: always moving, always having to start again, always presenting a new face to people.

'Then last summer we went back to England, where we spent some time with old friends and relations and all my neuroses disappeared. And I realized that my face looked whole. But when we came back, I felt it creeping back upon me, this feeling that I'm presenting a new face to everyone, every time, and that I've only got half a real face.

'Age is worrying, because each time I start in a new place I'm older. I shall now be touching forty. People don't know that I was once twenty. And in my mind I'm still in my twenties. When I see my friends in England, they don't think of age, they see me as I am - whole. But it's awful to think that each time I move the new people I meet see me as being my new age, as being only a small part of my real, my whole self.'

This feeling of estrangement from self is a symptom that is commonly experienced in stressful or alienating situations as well as certain psychological disorders. As such, it is not, of course, specific to expatriate wives; but because we encountered its description so frequently in the course of our research, it became to our minds symbolic of the identity problems that confront so many of them.

As many as 86% of the women in our survey said they had

experienced periods of depression which ranged from the temporary to the persistent. In conversations some of them reported they had suffered from agoraphobia, 'lump in the throat', apathy, psoriasis, vertigo, asthma, weight gain or loss and so on, all of which are, or can be, symptoms of depression, the sort of depression that may be associated with a form of mourning in which the loss is internal rather than external.

****

'I find', says Katherine, an American expatriate living in Brussels on a long-term basis, 'that people who move constantly retreat more and more into their shell of a family, and cling more and more to each other. And they are increasingly hesitant to put out their branches to the sunlight because they know it has to end again. They will only put down superficial roots because, if they're at all sensitive and start letting their roots go in deep, it will hurt to dig them up.

'I knew a woman who got so desperate about what constant moving did to her that her father, who was a New York psychiatrist, sent her plastic rose-bushes in plastic containers and she stuck these in her garden and took them along wherever she went.'

If the problem of roots is a crucial one for expatriates, it is also crucial for some of their contemporaries at home. Western society is today, as so many sociologists, philosophers, journalists have pointed out, the most mobile society that has ever existed. It is also the most temporary, the society most subject to transience, from the ephemerality of objects - we are known, after all, as the 'throwaway society' - and the fickleness of fashions, to the impermanence of places and relationships.

The imprint of mobility and change on our culture and the consequences for our basic human needs are profound. Writers, scientists, sociologists have written at length on the subject, and although it is not within the scope of this book to explore the phenomenon in any detail, it is important, in order to understand it to remember that the situation of professional expatriates must be viewed against its proper background - a world in motion, a world in which the notions of time, place, space, roots, no longer have the values they used to have.

Yet these are values that are still upheld as norms, and one of the great paradoxes of expatriate life is that, the more people move and the faster they move, the more they cling to the values of a permanent world. And what is their alternative, might you ask? What can they replace a feeling of 'belonging' with? How can they learn to renounce without bitterness the exercising of those rights that proclaim them to be part of a specific community and society? It is after all, says psychiatrist Robert Seidenberg, the exercising of those rights that 'changes existing into living.... To exert a meaningful influence on a community, one generally must have roots in it.... Gipsies and nomads are romantic and beautiful people, but history is clearly against them; those who merely pitch their tents have left little mark on civilization.' [1]

It is clear, when one attempts to view the situation of expatriates against its wider social context, that there are two processes at work. The first one results, directly or indirectly, from mobility and change as social phenomena. It expresses itself through feelings such as isolation, alienation, an acute sense of loss, a constant search for continuity, a lack of involvement with the environment, transience of friendships, lack of roots, and so on, and is common to both men and women.

The second process is one that is more specific to the expatriate wife in her role as the 'trailing spouse'. Here various factors come into play that contribute to what is often an overwhelming feeling of loss of control over her own life.

'Whither thou goest I will go' implies for many of the women who talked to us that they put their own wishes, priorities and goals in abeyance if these happen not to coincide with their husbands. In decisions such as the crucial one of following their spouse abroad or the no less crucial one of curtailing or changing their career to fit in with the demands of his, a large number of women felt that they had not exercised their own free will.

This inability to exercise one's free will can alone bring about a feeling of loss of power. But in the lives of many expatriate women it is reinforced by a number of other factors, linked with work, financial dependence and a new social status.

Of all these, as we saw in earlier chapters, it was the loss of their jobs or careers, their professional environment and the social recognition that goes with it that rankled most with a large number of expatriates.

The subject of complete financial dependence, which affected 65% of the women in our study, was also one that aroused strong feelings, not only among the women who, in their own country, had been economically independent, but also among women who had never worked, or who had stopped working some time before going abroad. In describing the feeling of helplessness that economic dependence aroused in them, many of these women referred to the notion of loss or lack of control over their own lives.

A further, and more insidious element that adds to this general feeling of helplessness is the very fact of being a 'trailing spouse' - a graphic term certain sociologists have bestowed on the wives (or husbands) who follow their mates in mobility - or a 'camp-follower' as some of the women in our study no less graphically described themselves.

These terms speak for themselves. They refer to people who, literally, 'follow' - i.e. who, by implication, do not lead, are not equally involved in decisions, come in second place.

If today fewer people than in the past are prepared to assert that a man's status is defined by what he does and a woman's by what her husband does, this definition is still applicable to the social situation of expatriate couples, and the mentality that goes with it pervades many aspects of expatriate life, from the social to the bureaucratic. 'What does your husband do?' is the classic opening phrase at social functions, and one which many of the women to whom we talked strongly objected to.

It is mostly, however, in tightly-knit, hierarchy-conscious communities such as the diplomatic service or the armed forces that the expatriate wife's vicarious status is really endemic. Not many women are strong enough or brave enough to resist the enormous pressure which a tradition of entrenched hierarchy and bureaucracy puts upon them. Among those who did resist was Alice, the wife of a Canadian official at S.H.A.P.E.

'The worst problem for me', she said when we interviewed her 'is the importance given to husbands' ranks. I was always sensitive about it, but in recent years it's become a *bête noire*. That's why I refuse to belong to women's groups here at S.H.A.P.E. You're supposed to put your husband's rank on any list, form or questionnaire you fill in, and I never do. Our official status is D.W. (Dependent Wife), and you're expected to put that, too, on any forms, on your I.D. card etc. I will agree to use the term "sponsored wife", though I prefer just "wife", but I absolutely refuse to put D.W. even if someone's standing over me while I'm doing it.

'The biggest adjustment I've had to make in thirty years of military life has to do with this. Now I don't object to hierarchy as a principle

- let's face it, everyone's got to have a boss - but I do object to my own status being dictated by my husband's. I find it degrading, and I've been battling for an official reviewing of the D.W. status. It's come up several times at official level and now it's being discussed, but it could be years before anything happens.'

Inability to exercise free will, loss of a professional environment, economic dependence, vicarious status - these obstacles to self-fulfillment can, of course, be encountered in any situation, anywhere: they are part of a wider system that has affected women at all times in all patriarchal societies and that still affects them to a large extent. Like other situations, however, this one is exacerbated and magnified by mobility and by the role women are called upon to play in it.

The situation many of the expatriate women in this book are facing is one of ambivalence and contradiction, which exists on two levels.

On a first level, that may be described as situational, many of these women are leading a life of greater material comfort and higher (though vicarious) social status than their contemporaries at home, while at the same time their own social status as professional or, at any rate, autonomous women has suffered a set back, and they find themselves gradually stripped of the tools and self-confidence that are needed in the increasingly competitive world to which, some day, they must return.

On a second level, which is deeper and has to do with a sense of self, these women are faced with contradictory expectations of attitude and behaviour: the expectations others have of them, and those they have of themselves. They are expected by others - their husbands, their children, their husbands' employers, the expatriate community at large - to play a warm, supportive role and place themselves last in the list of priorities; and this pressure is magnified by the fact that they themselves perceive that, for part of their time abroad at any rate, this role they are called upon to play may be vital to the well-being of their family.

Yet the expectations they have of themselves are those that a lot of women have fought for and gained in the last twenty-five years, and which, for many of them, consist of matters other than more money, househelp, a larger house, greater leisure - matters such as a feeling of belonging and involvement, professional achievement, social recognition as persons in their own right - in other words, self-fulfillment on their own terms.

This ambivalence is not always clearly perceived for, like all ambiguities, it tends to blur issues, and a lot of the women who expressed their dismay to us, admitted that they sometimes did not know where their true feelings lay. All of them, however, were conscious of a conflict within themselves, and one that generated feelings of anger and guilt.

A study of expatriate wives in Geneva blames this situation on the very nature of the international milieu which the authors describe as 'a uniquely modern form of patriarchy - diffuse, inaccessible, blameless and pervasive'. 'On the level of rhetoric', they say, 'it is an enlightened, progressive, rational and liberal body politic: few proponents of the enslavement of women can be found. In the area of civic rights it is apparently egalitarian.... In practice, it is a profoundly conservative milieu insofar as masculine values and sex-determined roles are imposed on everyone.' [2]

****

It is said that, as Gertrude Stein lay dying, she turned her face to the wall and said: 'What, then, is the answer?' Then, after a while, she added: 'But what is the question?'

Some of the women whose voices, experiences, feelings, we heard throughout the research for this book asked us whether the testimonies we had gathered had provided us with any answers. To which we often replied 'But what is the question?', only to find that many of these women had not fully formulated the question in their own minds. What they wanted was to be given reassurance, a key to happiness, an instant recipe for turning what is often a painful experience into a positive one.

And, indeed, what is the final question, for those expatriate women who are not at peace with their situation, for those others who have 'made the best of it' at some cost to themselves, for those who are weary of being carted from pillar to post but dare not interfere with their husbands' careers?

Is it a sombre echo of Edward Lear's words on his journey to Corsica - 'Am I not an idiot for coming at all?' Is it 'If I had to do it again, would I do it?' Is it 'Now that I'm here, what shall I do about it?' Is it 'Shall I go home and risk breaking up my marriage?' Is it 'Is it all worth it?' Is it 'Is there any recipe for developing portable roots? Or living without guilt? Or anger? Or sadness? Or resentment?'

Any attempt to answer such questions would be fatuous, because there *are* no answers we, or anybody else for that matter, can give those women. They have to find their own answers in the light of their own circumstances, the strength of their feelings, their commonsense, their relationship with their immediate family, and other elements which make each of their cases a unique one.

Similarly, any advice one might be tempted to give would necessarily fall short of people's expectations, because no amount of advice could cover the needs of all those different women. So we have largely refrained from giving direct advice and have chosen instead to present the testimonies, experiences and strategies of some of the women we met in the course of our research, in the hope that their examples might be of use to other women.

We have seen, from the case histories that started this book and from what women have said in the group discussions we reproduced, that it is often extremely difficult for some of them to unravel problems that are individual or relational, and independent of their situation as expatriates, from problems that may be the result of their moves abroad. It seems, therefore, important to stress once more the necessity for these women, as indeed for all expatriates who ask themselves questions, to try and put their individual situations in a broader perspective.

By setting these situations against the context of mobility as a widespread and ever increasing phenomenon of our age, and understanding the social and psychological mechanisms that this sets in motion, not only might they be able to sort out what is personal from what is the result of their situation as expatriates, but they might also feel less isolated in their doubts, frustration or unhappiness.

More generally so, it is only through a better understanding of those mechanisms that we, the new nomads and trailing spouses, may be able to fully accept the idea that we are moving figures in a moving landscape; that we have to learn to live with change, ambiguity, loss; to reassess all our old, inherited notions of permanence, place, belonging; to make a virtue out of contingency; to stop feeling guilty because we fear our children will grow up rootless; to develop - and help our children develop - truly portable roots, and find in ourselves that 'binding force' that formerly we expected, and received, from our home environment.

We started this book with the testimonies of three women. We have chosen to end it with the voice of one other, Lydia Horton*, whose years in Brussels have marked a whole generation of expatriate women.

---

*Own name used

LYDIA

Lydia is an American psychotherapist with a long experience of expatriate life. She now lives in the United States with her husband, Michael. When we interviewed her she was still living in Brussels.

'Looking back, I shudder when I think about how I got married. I was twenty-six and I realize now that I thought then I was over the hill. I was obviously responding to basic societal pressures, but they were pretty powerful pressures. Of course marrying on that basis led to constant difficulties in the marriage. In the same way, to me, having a family meant having four children: not until much later did I realize that I had four children because my mother had had four children.

'I finished college in 1942, just after the United States got into the war. I joined the Navy - Mrs Roosevelt had been round the colleges talking to the women about joining in the fighting, but by the time it got to Congress, they were saying things like "We can't have the flower of American womanhood going out of America."

'Then in 1946 I got a job with the U.S. embassy in Paris. It was a dumb job. I didn't intend to have a career in the foreign service - I just wanted to go abroad. Then I met Mike and we got married. I almost never went home again.

'We moved quite often - once to Swizerland, twice to Paris, twice to Belgium. We've been in Brussels twenty years. Wherever Mike's job went, I went. I had children in several languages and I know a great deal about comparative obstetric techniques. Every time we moved I felt I lost some of my identity. I would become "invisible" and have to re-invent myself. I found little half-ass jobs to do - nothing that was very rewarding or ever gave me any particular recognition. And I was miserable. I hated my life, I hated Mike, I hated myself. And I sort of trudged on like that.

'Eventually we landed in Brussels, and that was a big improvement, because I fell in with women who felt pretty much as I did, and we started talking. We began to realize, in fact, that we were not crazy. I had always felt that my pain, my anger and my paralysis were a product of my own inadequacies; so finding other women who felt the same way was very liberating for me; it gave me a great sense of comfort. By talking together and finding we had a lot in common, we realized that there was much about our situation that had nothing to do with our personal inadequacies, but had to do with the system we were inserted in, which was - and is -

very destructive to women. That was a great period for me, and it
saw the start of W.O.E.*

'All these things led me to question why so many intelligent, well-
educated women colluded with a system that was so destructive,
and I became interested in devising a kind of assertiveness training
that might be used as a tool to help women take more control of
their lives instead of forever feeling paralyzed, or disappointed, or
waiting for somebody else to make things better for them.

'I started experimenting, with my friends as guinea-pigs. The
results were so gratifying that they urged me to become professional. I read all the books I could get, but I felt I had to go back to
school and study the situation of women and the reasons for which
they get so paralyzed. I investigated the U.L.B.**, British universities, and found there was nothing there I could do. Then I found
an accredited institution in America that offered masters pro-
grammes in Europe. I presented my project to them, which was
eventually accepted as an M.A. thesis.'

Lydia spent the next few years writing her thesis and training as
a psychotherapist.

'Since then I have been slogging along, doing individual counselling, marriage therapy, courses and workshops on assertiveness
training. Every year I tried something new. There is so much to
learn when you start a new career so late in life. I want to try as
many things as I can. I have no intention of stopping. My great
luxury is taking two months in the summer to see my family - which
is very large - in the States.

'At some point I realized that a great deal more has been written
about women and their struggles to change than about men - or at
least those men who are the chosen partners and who choose to
remain the partners of these women in transition. Since their
partners are changing, they too are forced to change. So I devised
a workshop for men in transition.

'Originally I came here because of Mike but I would like to stay here
because this is where I have built up my job, and it so happens that
he retired and has chosen to stay here. Once I became self-
supporting I did not feel I had to follow him. One of the biggest
difficulties wives have has to do with the whole concept of following.
You are following somebody else's life, and whether you're moving
from city to city, state to state or country to country, you are
following, and you do not have control over your own life. You are
left with trying to put together whatever you can wherever you end

*Women's Organisation for Equality
**Université Libre de Bruxelles

up. You are constantly meeting someone else's professional career needs, not your own.

'One of the things that happened to me during my training and the therapy I had to undertake was that I renegotiated my relationship with Mike, and eventually I came to see that a lot of the things I blamed him for were really due to the system we're all operating under. It was then possible for me to absolve him, so to speak, of some of the blame I had previously focused on him.

'It also led me to disengage myself from him to a certain extent. I had been so vulnerable to criticism before, and we were always in contention with each other. Being economically independent meant a great deal to me. If we were in contention now, I feel I'd have the means to do what I thought was right. I had previously made *him* rather than myself the centre of so much of my expectations and discontent. When I arrived at a point where I felt a great deal better about myself, I started to feel a great deal better with him. I have now established quite a separate life from him, and now what we do together I do by choice, so it is a great deal pleasanter. We have done a lot of role reversal - he does the cooking now, for instance. We function more as friends than we ever did before. I no longer look to him for feedback - I get it elsewhere. And I have stopped feeling responsible for his feelings. This does not mean that I don't care: I just don't feel it is my job to make him happy; it is *his* job. I don't need sexual validation from men the way some women do. I think it distorts our awareness of ourselves.

'Change may well be occurring in the consciousness of expatriate wives, but at such a minuscule pace that we think it isn't. We are not going to meet a lot of pioneers here. The women I am working with are still coming up against the same problems as we did so many years ago. The assumption has always been that it is better to be married than not, and this is still the case.

'It is difficult in an expatriate situation, but, you know, I think it is difficult at home too. I came to the conclusion in my thesis that, however painful the experience of expatriate women is, it is very consciousness-raising, and had they stayed at home it might never have got to that point, although there might have been a lot of discontent just below the surface. So in some ways I think that it is a good thing for women to go abroad, face difficulties and be forced to reassess their life and where they are going.

'Even though for a lot of women the feminist revolution may have happened after they got married and gave up their jobs, it has not passed them by and how they lead their lives may be influenced by it. I feel that every woman alive today - whether she is my age, or your age, or younger - is in transition. Some of us are at different points in the spectrum, but we are all *in transition.*'

[1]. Seidenberg, Robert, *Corporate Wives, Corporate Casualities?*, New York, 1973.
[2]. Geneva Women's Cooperative, *op.cit.*

BIBLIOGRAPHY

The title, *Portable Roots*, was suggested by a sentence in Warren G. Bennis and Philip Slater's book, *The Temporary Society*, New York, 1969: 'I wrote that... the profession of wife in an era of change is to provide continuity, the portable roots.'

Among the books, articles and other publications we read, the following were useful:

ADINE, J.P. and MONROE, L., 'Les cadres français à l'étranger', *Le Point*, 23 June 1985.

ANDERSON, Michael (ed.), Sociology of the Family, *Harmondsworth*, 1971.

ARCHER, Clive, *International Organizations*, London, 1983.

ARMSTRONG, David, *The Rise of the International Organization*, London, 1982.

BADINTER, Elizabeth, *L'un est l'autre : des relations entre hommes et femmes*, Paris, 1986.

BAKER, James C., 'Company policies and executive wives abroad', in *Industrial Relations*, vol. 15, no.3, October 1976.

BAMFIELD, V. *On the Strength: The British Army Wife*, London, 1975.

BASTRESS, Frances, *The Relocating Spouse's Guide to Employment: Options and Strategies in the U.S. and Abroad*, Chevy Chase (Ma.), 1986.

BEAUVOIR, Simone de, *Le deuxième sexe*, Paris, 1949.

BOLLES, Richard Nelson, *What Color Is Your Parachute: A Practical Manual for Job-Hunters and Career Changers*, 1987.

BOTT, E., *Family and Social Network*, London, 1957.

CALLAN, H. 'The premiss of dedication: notes towards an ethno-graphy of diplomats' Wives', in Ardner, S. (ed.), *Perceiving Women*, London, 1975.

CENTRE D'ETUDES ET DE RECHERCHES URBAINES, *L'Europe à Bruxelles*, Brussels, 1982.

CHODOROW, Nancy, 'Family structure and feminine personality', in Rosaldo, M. and Lamphere, L. (eds.), *Woman, Culture and Society*, Stanford (Cal.), 1974.

COOPER, Cary L., *The Executive Gypsy*, New York, 1979.

COOPER, Cary L., *Executive Families under Stress*, New York, 1981.

COSER, Lewis A., *Greedy Organizations*, New York, 1974.

DOWLING, Colette, *The Cinderella Complex: Women's Hidden Fear of Independence*, London, 1982.

DSWA (Diplomatic Service Wives' Association) Magazine, London, various issues.

EDWARDS, J.N. (ed.), *The Family and Change*, New York, 1969.

ETZIONI, A. and E. (eds.), *Social Change*, New York, 1964.

FELL, Martine, *Ça va la famille?* Paris, 1983.

FEMMES D'EUROPE, published by the Commission of the European Communities particularly: *Les Femmes en chiffres; Femmes et hommes d'Europe en 1983*, and *Femmes au travail dans la Communauté européenne*.

FINCH, Janet, *Married to the Job: Wives' Incorporation in Men's Work*, London, 1983.

FOCUS Information Service, *A Resource for Expatriates in the U.K.*, various issues.

FORUM OF THE ASSOCIATION OF AMERICAN SERVICE WOMEN, various issues.

FRIEDAN, Betty, *The Second Stage*, New York, 1981.

FRIEZE, Irene H. *et al* (eds.), *Women and Sex Roles: A Social Psychological Perspective*, New York, 1978.

GENEVA WOMEN'S COOPERATIVE, *With Our Consent?*, Geneva, 1983.

GLASS, David C. (ed.), *Environmental Influences*, New York, 1968.

GOODE, W.J., *World Revolution and Family Patterns*, New York, 1963.

GOWLER, D. and LEGGE, K., 'Hidden and open contracts in marriage', in Rapoport R. and R.N. (eds.), *Working Couples*, London, 1978.

GREBER, Judith, *The Silent Partner*, London, 1985.

CROSS, Bertram M., *The Managing of Organizations* (2 vols), New York, 1964.

HANDY, C. *Understanding Organizations*, Harmondsworth, 1976.

Horton, Lydia Wells, *Displaced Women: A Study of the Problems of English-Speaking Women Resident in Europe and an Experiment in Re-Formation*, unpublished M.A. thesis, Goddard College, 1979.

HOUSE OF COMMONS PAPERS CMND 7294-7319, 1977-8.

JANEWAY, Elizabeth, *Man's World, Woman's Place: A Study in Social Mythology*, New York, 1971.

KANTER, Rosabeth Moss, *Men and Women of the Corporation*, New York, 1977.

KAPLAN, M.F. and GLENN, Ann, 'Women and the stress of moving: a self-help approach', in *Social Casework*, 1978.

LERNER, Daniel, *The Passing of Traditional Society*, New York, 1958.

LEVY, Michel Louis, *La Population de la France des années 80*, Paris, 1982.

MICHEL, Andrée, *Sociologie de la famille et du travail*, Paris, 1972.

MILLER, Jean Baker, *Towards a New Psychology of Women*, Harmondsworth, 1978.

MITCHELL, Juliet, *Women: The Longest Revolution*, London, 1984.

MOORHOUSE,G. *The Diplomats: The Foreign Office Today*, London, 1977.

MORRIS, J. *The 'Pax Britannica' trilogy (Heaven's Command; Pax Britannica; Farewell the Trumpets)*, Harmondsworth, 1979.

OAKLEY, Ann, *Housewife*, London, 1974.

      The Sociology of Housework, London, 1974.

      Subject Women, London, 1981.

PACKARD, Vance, *A Nation of Strangers*, New York, 1972.

PAHL, J. and R., *Managers and their Wives*, London, 1971.

PESKINE, Brigitte and ABERGEL, Micheline, *Femmes expatriées*, Paris, 1982.

PIERSON, George W., *The Moving American*, New York, 1972.

RAPOPORT, Rhona and Robert N., *Dual-Career Families Re-Examined*, London, 1976.

SCHOONMAKER, Alan N., *Anxiety and the Executive*, New York, 1969.

SEIDENBERG, Robert, *Corporate Wives, Corporate Casualties?*, New York, 1973.

      'Moving on to What?', in *Mental Hygiene*, Winter 1975.

SERVICE CANTONAL DE STATISTIQUES, GENEVE, *Données statistiques : Les Organisations internationales à Genève et en Suisse*, Geneva, 1987.

SHARPE, Sue, *Double Identity: The Lives of Working Mothers*, Harmondsworth, 1980.

SPEECKHAERST, G.P., *La Vie internationale en Belgique*, Brussels, 1980.

STEVENS, H, 'Women and the economics of family migration', in *Review of Economics and Statistics*, 1977.

SULLEROT, Evelyne, *Pour le meilleur et sans le pire*, Paris, 1984.

Woman, Society and Change, New York, 1974.

TOFFLER, Alvin, *Future Shock*, London, 1971.

The Third Wave, London, 1981.

TOWNSEND, Robert, *Up the Organization*, New York, 1970.

VARRO, Gabrielle, *La Femme transplantée : une étude du mariage franco-américain en France et le bilinguisme des enfants*, Lille, 1984.

WEISSMAN, Myrna M. and PAYKEL, Eugene S., 'Moving and Depression in women', Transaction/Society, July-August 1972.

WHYTE, William H., *The Organization Man*, Harmondsworth, 1960.

'The Wife Problem', in Epstein C.F. and Goode, W.J. (eds).

The Other Half: Roads to Women's Equality. Englewood Clifts (N.J.), 1971.

WOE, *Women's Opportunities Explored : Jobs and Education* Brussels, 1976.

ZWINGMANN, Charles (ed.), *Uprooting and After*, Berlin, Heidelberg and New York, 1973.